# The Essential Guide

# to

# Planning Your Dream

# Destination Wedding

**Expert Advice and Tips for
Your Perfect Destination Wedding**

**Karly Valentine**

# The Essential Guide
# to
# Planning Your Dream
# Destination Wedding

### Expert Advice and Tips for
### Your Perfect Destination Wedding

# Copyright

ISBN 979-8-9896898-3-5 (print)

EverCentury Books

# Disclaimer

The publisher and the author make no representation or warranties with respect to the accuracy or completeness of the contents of this work and specifically disclaim all warranties, including without limitation warranties of fitness for a particular purpose. No warranty may be created or extended by sales or promotional materials. The advice and strategies contained herein may not be suitable for every situation. This work is solid with the understanding that neither the publisher nor the author is engaged in rendering legal, accounting, or other professional services. If professional assistance is required, the services of a competent professional person should be sought. Neither the publisher nor the author shall be liable for damages arising here from. The fact that an organization or website is referenced in this work as a citation and/or a potential source of further information does not mean that the author or the publisher endorses the information the organization or website may provide or recommendations it may make. Further, readers should be aware that internet websites listed in this work may have changed or disappeared between the date this work was written and when it is read.

# Table of Contents

# Chapter 1
# Introduction and Checklists

## 1.1  Embracing the Romance of Destination Weddings

Welcome, lovebirds, wanderlusters, and adventure seekers alike, to the magical realm of destination weddings! If you've found yourself flipping through these pages, chances are you're not just dreaming of a traditional church ceremony followed by a reception in the same old banquet hall. No, you're yearning for something more – something exotic, whimsical, and downright unforgettable.

Picture this: a sun-kissed beach with powdery white sands stretching as far as the eye can see, the gentle lull of turquoise waves serenading your vows. Or perhaps you're envisioning a fairytale castle nestled amidst rolling hills, where history whispers secrets of romance and grandeur. Whatever your wildest wedding dreams may entail, one thing's for sure – you've caught the incurable wanderlust bug, and there's no turning back now!

But before you dive headfirst into the world of destination "I do's," allow me to be your trusty guide, your confidant in all things nuptial and nomadic. Together, we'll navigate the choppy seas of wedding planning, dodge the occasional rogue seagull (yes, they do tend to crash beach ceremonies), and uncover the hidden treasures of tying the knot in far-flung locales.

Now, I know what you're thinking: "Why on earth would I want to add the stress of planning a wedding to the already daunting task of organizing a vacation?" Fear not, dear reader, for I come bearing tales of romance, adventure, and the occasional mishap-turned-miracle. Trust me when I say that the journey to your dream destination wedding is not just about the destination itself – it's about the laughter shared, the tears shed, and the memories forged along the way.

So, grab your passport, pack your sense of adventure (and maybe a few extra bottles of sunscreen), and let's embark on this wild and wonderful adventure together. Destination weddings await, and the world is your oyster – with a side of champagne, of course. Cheers to love, laughter, and happily ever afters in the most extraordinary of places!

## 1.2    Checklist for Planning a Destination Wedding

Planning a destination wedding involves numerous details, from choosing the perfect locale to ensuring your guests have a memorable experience. This comprehensive checklist will guide you through the essential steps of planning your dream destination wedding.

### 12-18 Months Before

- ☐ Decide on a Budget: Establish a clear budget that includes all potential costs related to your destination wedding.
- ☐ Choose a Destination: Research and select a location that fits your vision, budget, and guests' needs.
- ☐ Visit the Destination (if possible): An initial visit can help you scout venues, meet vendors, and understand the local landscape.
- ☐ Select a Date: Consider local weather patterns, holidays, and peak tourist seasons when choosing your wedding date.

- ☐ Hire a Wedding Planner: Consider a local planner with expertise in destination weddings to help coordinate logistics and vendor communication.
- ☐ Book Your Venue: Secure your ceremony and reception locations.
- ☐ Create a Wedding Website: Include travel information, accommodations, itinerary, and other useful details for guests.

## 9-12 Months Before

- ☐ Send Save-the-Dates: Give guests plenty of notice to arrange travel and accommodations.
- ☐ Research Local Marriage Requirements: Understand the legal process for getting married in your chosen destination.
- ☐ Book Vendors: Secure key vendors such as photographers, caterers, florists, and entertainment.
- ☐ Arrange Accommodations: Block hotel rooms or recommend lodging options for your guests.
- ☐ Plan Guest Activities: Consider welcome events, group excursions, or other activities for guests.

## 6-9 Months Before

- ☐ Send Formal Invitations: Include RSVPs with a deadline to confirm guest numbers.
- ☐ Plan Your Menu: Work with your caterer to select dishes that reflect the local cuisine or your personal tastes.
- ☐ Choose Attire: Select wedding outfits suitable for the destination's climate and culture.
- ☐ Book Travel: Arrange flights and transportation for yourselves and confirm travel plans with guests.

### 3-6 Months Before

- ☐ Finalize Vendor Details: Confirm services, timelines, and any last-minute adjustments with your vendors.
- ☐ Purchase Wedding Bands: Choose and order your wedding rings.
- ☐ Arrange Transportation: Plan how guests will get from their accommodations to the wedding venue.
- ☐ Confirm Honeymoon Plans: Finalize bookings and itineraries for your honeymoon.

### 1-3 Months Before

- ☐ Finalize Guest List: Confirm who will be attending and finalize seating arrangements.
- ☐ Prepare Documentation: Ensure all legal documents, passports, and visas are in order for travel and marriage.
- ☐ Create a Day-Of Timeline: Outline the schedule for your wedding day, including ceremony, reception, and any other events.
- ☐ Pack Wisely: Start packing for the trip, including wedding attire, essentials, and any decorations or favors.

### Weeks Before

- ☐ Confirm Arrangements: Double-check bookings and arrangements with your venue and vendors.
- ☐ Communicate with Guests: Share the final itinerary, packing tips, and any last-minute details.
- ☐ Visit the Venue Again (if possible): A final visit can help finalize details and calm any pre-wedding nerves.

**Days Before**

- Arrive Early: Allow yourselves a few days in the destination before the wedding to handle any last-minute details and adjust to the time zone.
- Meet with Your Planner and Vendors: Review the final details and timeline to ensure everyone is aligned.
- Welcome Your Guests: Host a welcome event or informal gathering to thank your guests for coming.

**Day Of**

- Relax and Enjoy: Trust your planning and the professionals you've enlisted to bring your vision to life. Today is about celebrating your love and commitment to each other.

This checklist covers the key steps in planning a destination wedding, but remember, each wedding is unique. Adapt this guide to suit your personal vision and requirements, ensuring your special day is everything you've dreamed of and more.

## 1.3   Sample Timelines and Schedules

Creating a well-organized timeline and schedule is essential for ensuring your destination wedding unfolds smoothly. Below are sample timelines and schedules for your wedding day and the surrounding events, designed to keep everything on track and allow you and your guests to enjoy each moment to the fullest.

## Pre-Wedding Day Schedule

### Day Before the Wedding

### - Morning:
- 10:00 AM: Bridal party and family members arrive at the venue for a walk-through of the ceremony and reception sites.
- 11:30 AM: Final meeting with the wedding planner and key vendors to confirm details and timings.

### - Afternoon:
- 1:00 PM: Leisure time for guests, optional group activity or excursion.
- 3:00 PM: Spa appointments for relaxation and pampering.

### - Evening:
- 6:00 PM: Welcome dinner/reception for all guests. A casual event allowing everyone to mingle and relax.

## Wedding Day Timeline

### Morning:

- 8:00 AM: Bride and groom start their day with a light breakfast.

- 9:00 AM: Hair and makeup begin for the bride and bridal party.
- 10:00 AM: Groom and groomsmen start getting ready.
- 11:00 AM: Wedding planner checks in with vendors as they arrive and begin setup.

## Afternoon:

- 1:00 PM: First look and couple's photoshoot.
- 2:00 PM: Bridal party and family photos.
- 3:00 PM: Guests begin to arrive; welcome drinks served.
- 3:30 PM: Ceremony starts.
- 4:00 PM: Ceremony concludes; cocktail hour begins.

## Evening:

- 5:00 PM: Reception entrance and welcome speech.
- 5:30 PM: Dinner is served.
- 7:00 PM: First dance followed by open dancing.
- 8:00 PM: Cake cutting and dessert.
- 9:00 PM: Special surprise entertainment or activity.
- 10:00 PM: Late-night snacks or a food truck for guests.
- 11:00 PM: Reception officially ends; after-party begins for those who wish to continue celebrating.

## - Optional:
- Midnight send-off for the couple or a casual gathering for night owls.

## Post-Wedding Day Schedule

### Day After the Wedding

### - Morning:
- 9:00 AM: Farewell brunch for all guests. A relaxed event to thank everyone and say goodbyes.
- 11:00 AM: Optional group activity, like a sightseeing tour or a relaxed day at the beach.

### - Afternoon:
- Guests begin departures depending on their individual travel arrangements.
- Couple departs for their honeymoon or enjoys the rest of their stay.

## Notes for Effective Scheduling

- Flexibility: Build in extra time between events to accommodate any delays and ensure a relaxed pace.
- Communication: Share detailed schedules with your guests, bridal party, and vendors well in advance.
- Contingency Plans: Have backup plans for outdoor events in case of unfavorable weather conditions.
- Rest Periods: Ensure there are periods of downtime for you and your guests to rest and refresh.

Remember, these sample timelines and schedules are starting points. Tailor them to fit the unique flow and events of your wedding celebration, keeping in mind the needs and comfort of you and your guests. Effective scheduling is key to creating a memorable and enjoyable experience for everyone involved.

# Chapter 2
# Dreaming of a Destination Wedding

Once upon a time, in a land far, far away—well, actually, just a couple of clicks away on your Pinterest board—lies the dream of an enchanting destination wedding. It's where the sun kisses the sea, where mountains embrace the sky, or perhaps where ancient ruins whisper tales of eternal love. Welcome to the dreamy beginning of your wedding planning journey!

## 2.1   Why Choose a Destination Wedding?

Picture this: exchanging vows with the love of your life, with toes dipped in white sand or on a cliffside overlooking the vast ocean. Sounds like a scene from a romantic movie, right? That's the magic of a destination wedding. It's not just an event; it's an adventure—a unique experience that combines love, travel, and celebration into one incredible package. But why go through the hassle of planning an event miles away from home? Let's break it down, shall we?

A destination wedding is your canvas to paint memories against a backdrop of stunning landscapes. Whether it's the rugged cliffs of Ireland, the serene beaches of Bali, or the historic streets of New Orleans, these locations offer a magical atmosphere that can't be replicated back home. It's about giving your "I do" moment the grandeur—or the simplicity—it deserves, in a setting that elevates the experience beyond the ordinary.

Let's face it, trimming the guest list is one of the most daunting tasks in wedding planning. Opting for a destination wedding naturally filters your list to those willing and able to travel, resulting in a more intimate gathering. This isn't about exclusion but about celebrating your day with those who truly matter. It's the difference between a grand spectacle and a personal, meaningful celebration with your nearest and dearest.

Contrary to popular belief, destination weddings can be more cost-effective than traditional weddings. Many resorts and venues offer wedding packages that bundle services at a lower cost. Plus, with a smaller guest list, you can allocate your budget more generously towards creating an unforgettable experience for you and your guests, rather than covering the costs for a larger local wedding.

Imagine the luxury of stepping from your wedding reception directly into your honeymoon. No airports, no additional travel—just you, your partner, and the continuation of your celebration in paradise. Many couples choose a destination wedding not only for the wedding day itself but for the seamless transition into their honeymoon, saving both time and money, and extending the joy of the moment.

A destination wedding stands out from the traditional ceremony and reception. It reflects the couple's adventurous spirit, love for travel, or connection to a special place. This unique celebration is a chance to break free from the expected and craft a day that's as unique as your love story. From local traditions and cuisine to breathtaking venues, your wedding will be anything but cookie-cutter.

For your guests, attending your destination wedding is not just about witnessing your union but also about enjoying a mini-vacation themselves. It's an opportunity for them to explore a new place, experience different cultures, and make memories that extend beyond the wedding day. Your wedding becomes a memorable getaway for everyone involved, creating stories and bonds that last a lifetime.

While planning a wedding from afar might seem daunting, many destinations offer dedicated wedding planners who specialize in organizing events for out-of-town couples. These experts help streamline the planning process, from navigating legal requirements to coordinating local vendors, making it easier for you to enjoy the journey to your big day.

Destination wedding is a beautiful blend of travel, adventure, and romance, offering a start to your married life that is as unique and extraordinary as your relationship. So, if your heart yearns for a wedding that breaks the mold, consider setting your sights on a destination that speaks to you, and let the adventure begin.

## 2.2    Popular Wedding Destinations Around the World

Ah, the million-dollar question: where to take your love story on a global adventure? From sun-drenched beaches to majestic mountaintops, the world is bursting at the seams with dreamy destinations just waiting to host your big day. So, let's grab our metaphorical passports and embark on a whirlwind tour of some of the most sought-after wedding spots across the globe!

**Beach Bliss:**
Picture-perfect palm trees swaying in the breeze, crystal-clear waters stretching as far as the eye can see – it's no wonder that beach weddings remain a perennial favorite among couples looking to tie the knot in paradise. From the sun-kissed shores of the Caribbean to the idyllic islands of Hawaii and the exotic allure of Thailand, beach destinations offer a winning combination of romance, relaxation, and barefoot bliss.

**European Elegance:**

For those craving a dash of old-world charm and sophistication, Europe beckons with its timeless beauty and fairy tale settings. Imagine exchanging vows amidst the rolling vineyards of Tuscany, the historic streets of Paris, or the ancient castles of Scotland. With its rich cultural heritage, stunning architecture, and mouthwatering cuisine, Europe provides a magical backdrop for couples seeking a wedding steeped in history and romance.

**Urban Chic:**

Who says you need to escape to the countryside or the beach to have a picture-perfect wedding? For city slickers and cosmopolitan couples alike, urban destinations offer a plethora of chic and stylish venues to say "I do." From the iconic skylines of New York City and Tokyo to the quaint cobblestone streets of Prague and the vibrant markets of Marrakech, the world's metropolises are brimming with possibilities for a wedding that's as unique and vibrant as you are.

**Off-the-Beaten-Path:**

Dare to be different and discover the hidden gems and under-the-radar destinations that promise to make your wedding truly unforgettable. Whether you're exchanging vows atop a glacier in Iceland, amidst the vine-covered hills of New Zealand, or in a rustic farmhouse in the countryside of Brazil, off-the-beaten-path destinations offer a sense of adventure and discovery that's sure to leave a lasting impression on you and your guests.

So there you have it – a tantalizing glimpse into the world of popular wedding destinations around the globe. Whether you're dreaming of sandy shores, historic landmarks, bustling cities, or remote hideaways, the perfect wedding destination is out there just waiting to be discovered. So pack your bags, practice your vows, and get ready to embark on the adventure of a lifetime!

For a comprehensive list of popular destinations, along with their pros and cons, please refer to the Appendix at the end of this book.

## 2.3   Understanding the Unique Charm of Each Location

Every destination holds a unique charm, an essence that can transform your wedding into a deeply personal and unforgettable celebration. But what makes each location special? It's not just the scenic beauty; it's the soul of the place—the culture, the landscapes, the flavors, and the traditions that breathe life into your special day.

For instance, a wedding in Italy might involve a quaint vineyard ceremony followed by a reception featuring the finest pasta dishes. Meanwhile, a ceremony in Thailand could see you riding in on an elephant, exchanging vows in a lush jungle setting, and feasting on spicy local delicacies. Each destination offers a distinct flavor, both literally and figuratively.

Remember, a destination wedding is more than just a day; it's an immersive experience for you and your guests. It's about stepping into a different world, where every detail tells a part of your love story. Whether it's through the local cuisine, the traditional music, or the breathtaking landscapes, your wedding will be a fusion of your personalities and the essence of the destination.

Let's dive into the art of understanding and embracing the unique charm of each location.

### The Heartbeat of Culture

Imagine a wedding in Italy, where the rich tapestry of art, history, and culinary excellence sets the stage for your love story. Or picture a traditional Hawaiian ceremony, with the sound of the ocean, the warmth of the sand, and the spirit of Aloha enveloping you and your guests. Each destination has its own cultural heartbeat, a rhythm that influences everything from the ceremony to the celebration. By choosing a location, you're inviting its culture to become a part of your wedding, offering an experience that's deeply rooted in the local way of life.

### The Canvas of Landscapes

From the rugged coastlines of Ireland to the serene rice fields of Bali, the landscape of your wedding destination adds a natural beauty and drama to your celebration. These landscapes aren't just backgrounds for stunning photos; they're active participants in your wedding. They set a tone, evoke emotions, and create an atmosphere that's impossible to replicate. Understanding the landscapes of your chosen destination allows you to align your wedding theme and decor with the natural surroundings, ensuring a harmonious and immersive experience.

### The Palette of Flavors

Local cuisine is a reflection of a destination's history, geography, and culture. By incorporating local dishes and ingredients into your wedding menu, you're not just offering a meal; you're providing a taste of the destination's soul. Imagine a beach wedding in Mexico with a feast featuring fresh seafood, vibrant salsas, and tequila-infused cocktails. Or a countryside wedding in France, where the wine flows as freely as the conversations, and every course is a tribute to French culinary prowess. Understanding and embracing these flavors allows you to craft a culinary experience that's as memorable as the vows you exchange.

## The Rhythm of Traditions

Every destination carries its own set of traditions and customs, which can add depth and meaning to your wedding ceremony and celebration. Whether it's incorporating a traditional Maori Haka in New Zealand, releasing lanterns into the night sky in Thailand, or stomping on a glass in a Jewish ceremony, these traditions connect your wedding to something larger—a history, a community, a shared humanity. Engaging with these traditions respectfully can add layers of significance and emotion to your celebration, creating moments that resonate with everyone involved.

## Embracing the Local Environment

Understanding a location's unique charm also means acknowledging and adapting to its environmental conditions. A midday beach wedding in the Caribbean? Beautiful, but potentially hot and humid. An evening ceremony in the mountains of Colorado? Breathtaking, but chilly. By embracing the local environment, you can plan your wedding logistics to ensure comfort and enjoyment for you and your guests, from choosing the right time of day to selecting attire that suits the climate.

## Real-Life Experience:

Let me tell you about Sarah and Alex, who dreamt of a wedding that combined their love for travel and adventure. They chose a quaint little island in Greece, known for its stunning sunsets and crystal-clear waters. Their guests were treated to a taste of Greek hospitality, with a pre-wedding tour of ancient ruins and a traditional feast that had everyone attempting to dance the Sirtaki by the end of the night.

But here's a word of advice from their experience: always check the local holidays. They accidentally scheduled their wedding on the same weekend as a major festival. Turns out, sharing your wedding with a thousand extra revelers in the streets can be quite the party—though securing a quiet moment for the ceremony proved to be a challenge worthy of Hercules.

As you dream of your destination wedding, remember that it's all about creating a unique celebration that reflects your journey together. So, let your imagination soar, explore the endless possibilities, and get ready for the adventure of a lifetime.

And with that, you're one step closer to not just marrying the love of your life but doing so in a way that will have your friends and family talking for years to come—assuming, of course, they make the guest list.

# Chapter 3
# Planning Your Destination Wedding

Congratulations! You've dreamt of a destination wedding and decided to embark on the adventure of a lifetime. Now, it's time to turn those dreams into reality. Planning a destination wedding can seem like navigating a ship through unknown waters, but fear not. With the right map and compass, you'll find your way to a breathtaking celebration that reflects your love story. Let's dive into the essentials of planning your destination wedding, one step at a time.

## 3.1    Initial Considerations and Setting a Date

Embarking on the journey of planning a destination wedding starts with foundational decisions that will shape the entire experience. Among these, selecting the perfect date stands as a pivotal choice, intertwined with various initial considerations that warrant careful thought and planning. Here's a guide to navigate these initial steps, ensuring your destination wedding is as seamless and memorable as possible.

### Understanding Your Vision

Before diving into logistics, take a moment with your partner to envision what your ideal wedding looks like. Are you imagining a beach ceremony with the sound of waves as your soundtrack, or a quaint chapel in a historic European town? Your vision will not only influence your choice of destination but also the timing of your wedding.

## Considering the Destination's Climate

The climate of your chosen destination will significantly affect your wedding date. Research the best time to visit, taking into account factors like weather conditions, peak tourist seasons, and local holidays. For instance, a Caribbean beach wedding is ideal during the dry season, while a Tuscan villa wedding might be best in late spring or early autumn to avoid the scorching summer heat and the tourist rush.

## Guest Availability and Convenience

The date of your wedding impacts not just you but also your guests, especially for a destination event. Consider school holidays, major holidays, or any dates that might conflict with significant events in your guests' lives. Early communication is key; sending out save-the-dates or a preliminary survey can help gauge availability and ensure those you love can be there to celebrate with you.

## Budget Implications

The timing of your wedding can also affect your budget. Peak tourist seasons often mean higher prices for flights, accommodations, and even venue rentals. Opting for a shoulder season—just before or after peak tourist times— can offer a balance of good weather, fewer crowds, and more favorable rates.

## Legal and Logistical Considerations

Some destinations have specific legal requirements or paperwork processing times for weddings, which can influence your date choice. For example, certain countries require a minimum residency period before the ceremony. Additionally, consider the logistics of your chosen location, such as accessibility for guests traveling from afar and any local events that might affect travel or accommodation availability.

### Balancing Significance and Practicality

While practical considerations are crucial, you might also want to think about dates that hold personal significance. Perhaps you'd like to marry on the anniversary of when you met, or a date that honors a loved one. Balancing these sentimental choices with the practical aspects mentioned can lead you to a date that feels both meaningful and wisely chosen.

### Flexibility and Openness

Finally, approach your date selection with flexibility and openness. While you might have an ideal date in mind, being willing to adjust based on your venue's availability, budget considerations, or guest needs can lead to discovering a date that's even more perfect than you initially imagined.

## 3.2   Budgeting for Your Destination Wedding

Embarking on the journey of a destination wedding is akin to setting sail into the sunset—romantic, adventurous, and, let's be honest, requiring a well-planned budget to avoid getting lost at sea. Budgeting for your destination wedding is not just about keeping costs under control; it's about smartly allocating your resources to create a magical day that reflects your love story without sinking your finances. Let's navigate through the key elements of budgeting for your destination wedding, ensuring your voyage to marital bliss is both splendid and financially savvy.

### Understand the Full Scope of Your Budget

Begin by setting a clear overall budget, considering every potential expense from the get-go. Destination weddings often include costs that traditional weddings might not, such as travel expenses for the couple, accommodations, welcome bags for guests, and activities outside of the wedding day itself. A thorough understanding of your budget's scope will help you prioritize what's most important and where you can be more flexible.

### Factor in Destination-Specific Costs

Every destination has its unique cost considerations. Research the local economy of your chosen location to get a sense of prices for services like catering, photography, and venue rental. Don't forget to account for currency exchange rates, which can significantly affect your budget. Additionally, consider the logistics of your chosen locale—remote or hard-to-reach destinations may incur higher transportation and accommodation costs.

### Travel and Accommodation Strategies

Your and your guests' travel and accommodations will likely be a significant portion of your budget. Look for group rates on flights and hotels, or consider renting large villas or homes to house guests, which can be more cost-effective and create a more intimate experience. Some couples opt to cover a portion of their guests' accommodation costs as a gesture of appreciation for making the journey, so consider if and how this might fit into your budget.

### Vendor and Venue Selection

Choosing Your Crew Wisely: The vendors and venue you select can dramatically impact your budget. Resorts and hotels often offer all-inclusive wedding packages that bundle services at a lower cost, simplifying your planning process. However, if you opt for an independent venue, you'll need to hire vendors individually, which might offer more personalized options but requires careful budget management. Always negotiate and ask for detailed quotes to avoid unexpected costs.

**Plan for the Unexpected**

A wise sailor always prepares for unforeseen conditions. Set aside a portion of your budget as a contingency fund, typically around 10-15%, to cover unexpected expenses or last-minute changes. Whether it's weather-related issues, vendor cancellations, or additional decor needs, having a financial buffer will ensure you can navigate any surprises without panic.

**Consider Additional Celebrations**

One of the joys of a destination wedding is the opportunity to embrace the local culture, which can also be a budget saver. Consider incorporating local flowers, foods, and entertainment into your wedding, which not only adds authenticity and charm but can also be more cost-effective than importing goods or talent.

## 3.3    Unveiling the Cost by Categories

While the allure of a barefoot ceremony on a pristine beach is undeniable, destination weddings come with a unique set of financial considerations. To help you navigate the costs and create a realistic budget, here's a breakdown of the major expense categories for your destination wedding:

**Travel & Accommodations (40-50% of total budget)**

This is often the biggest chunk of your destination wedding budget. Here's what to consider:

- **Flights**: Costs will vary depending on the destination, seasonality, and how far in advance you book. Book early and look for deals and packages.

- **Accommodation**: Research various options like hotels, all-inclusive resorts, vacation rentals, or boutique properties. All-inclusive resorts can simplify planning and potentially save money, but compare prices with individual bookings.
- **Guest Transportation**: Factor in costs of airport transfers, taxis, shuttles, or car rentals for your guests depending on the location and layout of your chosen destination.

## Wedding Ceremony & Reception (20-30% of total budget)

This covers your dream venue and the celebration itself:

- **Venue Rental**: Costs will vary depending on the location, size, and type of venue (beachfront resort, historical building, vineyard). All-inclusive resorts might bundle ceremony and reception space within their packages.
- **Catering**: Food and beverage costs can be significant. Research catering options offered by your venue or explore local vendors. Consider reception styles like buffets or plated meals to manage costs.
- **Décor**: Flowers, draping, centerpieces, and other decorative elements can add up quickly. Explore DIY options or consider using natural elements found at your destination.
- **Entertainment**: Live music, a DJ, or other entertainment options can add a festive touch, but factor in their fees when budgeting.

## Attire (10-15% of total budget)

While destination weddings might allow for lighter and more relaxed attire, don't underestimate the costs:

- **Wedding Outfits**: Factor in the cost of your wedding dress or suit, any necessary alterations, and accessories.
- **Guest Attire**: While guests will likely choose more casual attire, consider if any specific attire requirements might impact their budget.

## Legalities & Documentation (5-10% of total budget)

- **Marriage License:** Fees vary depending on the destination. Research and budget accordingly.
- **Documentation**: Some countries might require additional paperwork like visas or passport validations. Factor in any associated costs.

## Photography & Videography (10-15% of total budget)

- **Capturing Memories**: Professional photography and videography can be an investment. Research local vendors and compare packages to find one that fits your needs and budget.

## Remember:

- **Unexpected Costs**: Allocate a buffer in your budget for unforeseen expenses like tipping, travel insurance, or last-minute alterations.

- **Prioritize & Allocate**: Identify your non-negotiables (dream venue, photography) and allocate your budget accordingly. Explore ways to save on other aspects like décor or entertainment.

**The Next Step:**

With a breakdown of these major cost categories, you can start creating a realistic budget for your destination wedding. The following chapters will delve deeper into budgeting strategies, navigating guest logistics, and finding the perfect vendors for your dream day.

## 3.4 Financial Responsibilities: Who Pays for What in a Destination Wedding

Navigating the financial waters of a destination wedding can feel like charting unknown territory. With guests traveling from afar to celebrate your special day, understanding the etiquette around who pays for what is crucial. This clarity helps manage expectations, fosters goodwill, and ensures that both the couple and their guests are comfortable with the arrangements. Let's explore the traditional financial responsibilities and modern adaptations in the context of a destination wedding.

### The Couple's Responsibilities
- Wedding Essentials: Traditionally, the couple (or their families, depending on the arrangements) covers the cost of the wedding ceremony and reception. This includes venue rental, decorations, catering, entertainment, photography, and any other vendors directly related to the wedding day festivities.

- Wedding Party Expenses: It's a kind gesture for the couple to consider contributing to the attire, accommodation, or travel expenses of the wedding party. While not obligatory, offering to pay for or subsidize bridesmaids' dresses, groomsmen's attire, or accommodations is increasingly common, especially if specific attire or stay arrangements are requested.

- Welcome and Farewell Gatherings: Hosting a welcome party and a farewell brunch where all guests are invited is a customary expense borne by the couple. These events enhance the guest experience and provide additional opportunities to celebrate together.

## Guest Responsibilities

- Travel and Accommodation: Guests typically cover their own travel expenses, including airfare, accommodations, and personal expenses throughout their stay. The couple can facilitate this by negotiating group rates for flights and hotels and providing detailed travel information.

- Additional Activities: If guests choose to participate in optional activities outside the wedding itinerary (such as excursions, tours, or extra days of stay), they would cover these expenses themselves.

## Shared Costs and Considerations

- Transportation to Events: Providing shuttle service or group transportation from the accommodation to the wedding venue and back is often arranged and paid for by the couple, ensuring guests' safety and convenience.

- Meals Outside Wedding Events: Guests are generally expected to pay for their meals outside of the official wedding events. However, the couple might choose to organize and cover additional group meals or gatherings as part of the festivities.

## Modern Etiquette and Flexibility

- Transparent Communication: The key to managing expectations around finances is clear and open communication. Include information on your wedding website and in your invitations about what costs guests can anticipate.

- Understanding Financial Constraints: Be empathetic to guests' financial situations. Some may not be able to afford the trip. Consider ways to include them in local celebrations before or after the destination wedding.

- Personalized Contributions: Every couple and their financial situation are unique. Some may choose to cover more costs for their guests, especially for close family members or the wedding party, to ease the financial burden of attending.

## 3.5  Choosing the Right Venue: Resorts vs. Independent Venues

The venue for your destination wedding sets the stage for your entire event. Resorts often provide all-inclusive wedding packages that simplify planning from afar. These packages can include everything from the ceremony setup to accommodations for guests. However, if you crave a more personalized and unique experience, consider independent venues like historic estates, private villas, or even a vineyard. Each offers distinct charms but may require more effort to coordinate vendors and logistics.

### Resorts: All-Inclusive Elegance

Many offer all-inclusive wedding packages that take care of virtually every aspect of your wedding—from the ceremony and reception to flowers, photography, and even legal paperwork. For couples looking to streamline their planning process, especially from afar, resorts present a hassle-free option.

With amenities like spas, restaurants, and entertainment, resorts ensure that both you and your guests have everything needed for a memorable stay. This can be particularly appealing for weddings that double as a vacation for your guests, offering them a plethora of activities and services at their doorstep.

Resorts often provide more bang for your buck. The bundling of services in a package can lead to savings compared to sourcing each service individually. Furthermore, resorts may offer room discounts for you and your guests, adding to the financial appeal.

While resorts offer convenience, some couples find the packages a bit too cookie-cutter, limiting the personalization of their big day. However, many resorts are willing to customize aspects of their packages if you negotiate or if you're willing to pay a bit extra for certain bespoke elements.

### Independent Venues: Unique and Personalized
Independent venues, such as villas, castles, wineries, or even private beaches, provide a unique and unforgettable setting for your wedding. They offer a charm and individuality that can make your wedding stand out, reflecting your personal taste and story.

One of the biggest draws of independent venues is the ability to customize every aspect of your wedding. From choosing your own caterer to decorating the space exactly as you envision, independent venues offer the flexibility to bring your dream wedding to life without the constraints of a package deal.

Independent venues often provide the option for exclusivity—meaning your wedding party will be the only guests on site. This can create a more intimate and personal atmosphere, making your big day feel even more special.

While the freedom of an independent venue is appealing, it comes with the responsibility of managing multiple vendors and coordinating every detail yourself or with the help of a wedding planner. This can be more time-consuming and may require more effort, especially if you're planning from abroad.

With independent venues, every element is itemized, which can help you understand exactly where your money is going. While this can sometimes be more expensive than a bundled resort package, it also means you only pay for what you truly want.

### Making the Decision
When deciding between a resort and an independent venue for your destination wedding, consider what matters most to you and your partner. Are you looking for the

convenience and ease of a resort, or do you prioritize the uniqueness and flexibility of an independent venue? Reflect on your wedding vision, budget, and how much planning you're willing to undertake.

Remember, whether you choose the luxurious ease of a resort or the personalized charm of an independent venue, the most important thing is that the location speaks to your heart. After all, your wedding venue is more than just a place—it's where you'll celebrate one of the happiest days of your life.

## 3.6    Legal Requirements for Getting Married Abroad

Marrying in a foreign country comes with its own set of legal intricacies. From marriage licenses to residency requirements, ensure you understand what's needed well in advance. While the idea of legally tying the knot in a foreign country might seem romantically appealing, it often comes with a set of challenges and complexities that can add stress to your wedding planning. Here's a look at why obtaining your marriage license in your home country before heading to your overseas wedding location might be the preferable choice.

### Legal Requirements and Documentation

Countries have varying legal requirements for marriage, including residency periods, specific documentation, and sometimes even medical tests. Navigating these requirements can be daunting, especially with language barriers.

The United States has a more standardized process for obtaining a marriage license, with requirements being more straightforward and consistent across states. This can simplify the legal aspect of your wedding.

**Simplifying the Process**

By getting legally married here, you avoid the potential bureaucracy and paperwork involved with international marriages. This can include the need to have documents translated and legalized, which can be both time-consuming and costly.

Opting for a symbolic ceremony at your destination allows you to focus on personalizing your celebration without worrying about fulfilling legal obligations during your wedding. The legal marriage can be a simple affair back home, with the destination wedding fully dedicated to celebrating your union with loved ones.

**Recommendations for a Smooth Process**

Consider having a civil ceremony in your home state to take care of the legal aspects of your marriage. This can be a private moment or shared with close family and friends, separate from your destination celebration.

Research the requirements for obtaining a marriage license in your state, including any waiting periods or documents needed. This ensures you're legally married before you depart for your destination wedding.

If navigating the legal requirements seems overwhelming, consider consulting with a legal professional or a wedding planner who specializes in destination weddings. They can offer valuable guidance and ensure you've met all necessary legalities for your marriage to be recognized.

With the legalities taken care of, you can plan your destination wedding as a symbolic celebration of your love. This allows you to incorporate local customs, traditions, and the beautiful backdrop of your chosen destination into your ceremony without the stress of legal requirements.

# Chapter 4
# All-Inclusive Destination Wedding

## 4.1   The Allure of an All-Inclusive Destination Wedding

The allure of an all-inclusive destination wedding lies in its simplicity, beauty, and comprehensive nature, making it an increasingly popular choice among couples looking to tie the knot. This approach offers a streamlined planning process, allowing couples to focus more on the excitement of their upcoming union and less on the intricacies of wedding planning. Below, we delve into the specific aspects that make all-inclusive destination weddings so appealing.

### Simplified Planning
The most significant advantage of an all-inclusive destination wedding is the simplification of the planning process. Couples are spared the daunting task of coordinating every detail separately — from catering to decorations to entertainment. Instead, they select a package that fits their vision, and the venue handles the rest. This consolidation significantly reduces the stress and time involved in planning, making the lead-up to the wedding more enjoyable for the couple.

### Cost-Effectiveness
Contrary to what one might assume, all-inclusive weddings can be more budget-friendly than traditional weddings. With all major expenses bundled into one package, couples can easily monitor their spending and

avoid the hidden costs that often accompany separately booked services. Furthermore, many resorts and venues offer a variety of packages to suit different budgets, ensuring that couples can find an option that allows them to celebrate their love without breaking the bank.

## Stunning Locations

All-inclusive weddings are often held at breathtaking destinations around the world. Whether it's a beachfront ceremony in the Caribbean, a rustic affair in the Tuscan countryside, or a romantic exchange of vows in a French château, these weddings provide a backdrop that adds an element of unforgettable magic to the occasion. The beauty of these locations not only enhances the wedding itself but also offers an extraordinary setting for wedding photography, capturing memories that will last a lifetime.

## Convenience for Guests

For guests, the convenience of an all-inclusive wedding cannot be overstated. Accommodations, festivities, and often additional activities are located in one place, eliminating the need for guests to navigate foreign locations on their own. This setup not only facilitates a smoother experience for those attending but also encourages more guests to make the trip, knowing their stay will be hassle-free.

## Personalized Experiences

Despite being package-based, many all-inclusive weddings are highly customizable. Couples can work with on-site wedding coordinators to tailor aspects of their celebration to their preferences, ensuring their wedding day reflects their personal style and love story. From floral arrangements and menu selections to music and entertainment, the flexibility of these packages allows for personal touches that make the day uniquely theirs.

### Comprehensive Services

Beyond the ceremony and reception, all-inclusive packages often include additional services that enhance the wedding experience. These can range from pre-wedding spa treatments for the couple to organized activities for guests, adding layers of enjoyment to the celebration. Moreover, the presence of a dedicated wedding coordinator ensures that all details, big and small, are managed professionally, allowing the couple to relax and fully immerse themselves in their special day.

## 4.2    Assessing Your Needs and Preferences

When considering an all-inclusive destination wedding, assessing your needs and preferences is a crucial first step to ensuring your special day aligns perfectly with your vision and expectations. This assessment covers various aspects, from the type of setting you envision to the level of customization you desire, ensuring that your wedding is not only a reflection of your love but also a celebration that feels uniquely yours. Here's a closer look at how to assess your needs and preferences effectively.

### Envisioning the Setting

Begin by envisioning the ideal backdrop for your wedding. Do you dream of a beach ceremony with the sound of waves gently crashing in the background, or do you prefer the rustic charm of a countryside villa? Perhaps the elegance of a historic castle fits your fairy-tale wedding. Considering the setting is the first step in narrowing down your destination choices, ensuring that your wedding atmosphere aligns with your personal style and preferences.

### Determining Guest Considerations

Think about who you want to share your special day with. Assessing your guest list early on can help determine the size and scope of your wedding, as well as any specific accommodations your guests might need. Consider whether your preferred destination is accessible and enjoyable for all your guests, including those with mobility issues or families with children. The right all-inclusive package will offer a balance of fun and convenience for guests of all ages.

### Evaluating Budget Constraints

Budget is a pivotal factor in planning a destination wedding. All-inclusive packages can offer significant savings by bundling services, but it's essential to evaluate what's included and whether there are any potential extra costs. Consider what elements of your wedding are non-negotiable and where you might be willing to compromise. Understanding your financial boundaries will help you select a package that offers the best value without sacrificing the elements most important to you.

### Customization and Personal Touches

While all-inclusive packages provide ease and convenience, ensure there's room for personalization. Whether it's the color scheme, menu options, or floral arrangements, your ability to customize these elements can make your wedding feel more personal. Discuss with potential venues or planners about how they accommodate customization within their packages. Knowing that you can tailor aspects of your wedding package to suit your style can significantly influence your venue choice.

**Quality and Scope of Services**

Assess the quality and scope of services included in the package. This includes everything from the expertise of the on-site wedding coordinator to the caliber of the culinary offerings and the entertainment options. Research reviews or request testimonials from past couples to gauge the level of service provided. Additionally, consider any unique services that might enhance your wedding experience, such as exclusive activities for guests or special bridal spa packages.

**Flexibility and Contingency Planning**

Understand the venue's flexibility and policies regarding contingency planning, especially for outdoor weddings. Weather can be unpredictable, and having a solid plan B is essential. Inquire about the venue's experience in handling unforeseen circumstances and how they ensure the celebration goes smoothly, regardless of external factors.

**Legal and Logistical Considerations**

Finally, consider the legal and logistical aspects of marrying abroad. Different countries have varying requirements for legal marriage, so it's crucial to understand what's needed to ensure your marriage is recognized both in your destination country and at home. Also, think about the logistics of planning from afar and how the venue supports couples in navigating these challenges.

## 4.3    Finding Your Best All-Inclusive Destination Wedding Venues

With the vast array of options available online, it's essential to approach this task methodically to ensure that your special day is as magical as envisioned. Here's a comprehensive guide to researching, comparing, and finding the best all-inclusive destination wedding venues online.

### Define Your Wedding Vision

Before diving into the sea of online resources, take a moment to envision your ideal wedding. Consider the setting, size, and style you desire. Whether you dream of a tropical beach ceremony or a quaint European affair, having a clear vision will streamline your search and help you focus on venues that align with your aspirations.

### Research Potential Destinations

Start by exploring destinations that cater to all-inclusive weddings. Websites like Destination Weddings offer a wealth of information on various locations and packages. Consider factors such as climate, accessibility for guests, and legal requirements for marriage in each destination.

### Compare All-Inclusive Packages

All-inclusive packages can significantly simplify wedding planning by bundling services like catering, decorations, and entertainment. However, not all packages are created equal. Compare offerings from different resorts and venues to determine which provides the best value and aligns with your needs. Resources like Paradise Weddings provide insights into the best all-inclusive wedding packages available.

### Consult with Wedding Specialists

Engaging with a Destination Wedding Specialist can be invaluable. These professionals have in-depth knowledge of various destinations and can offer personalized recommendations based on your preferences and budget.

They can also assist in navigating the complexities of planning a wedding abroad.

## Check Reviews and Testimonials

Reading reviews from couples who have experienced the venues firsthand can offer a realistic perspective on what to expect. Look for testimonials on the venue's website or on wedding forums. Pay attention to comments about the quality of service, accommodations, and overall satisfaction.

## Virtual Tours and Galleries

Many venues now offer virtual tours or extensive photo galleries online. Take advantage of these to get a feel for the venue's ambiance and facilities. It's a great way to narrow down your choices without having to travel to each location.

## Contact Venues Directly

Once you've shortlisted your top venues, reach out to them directly. Inquire about availability, package customization options, and any special promotions they might offer. This direct communication can also give you a sense of the venue's customer service quality.

## Make an Informed Decision

After thorough research and comparison, you'll be equipped to make an informed decision. Choose the venue that not only meets your criteria but also feels right. Trust your instincts and look forward to the beautiful journey ahead.

## 4.4    What's Included in All-Inclusive Wedding Packages

All-inclusive wedding packages are designed to streamline the planning process and provide nearly everything you need for your special day under one cost structure. These packages can vary widely from venue to venue, but they typically include the essentials of wedding planning along with some extras that can elevate your experience. Understanding what's generally included will help you assess the value and determine if an all-inclusive package meets your needs and vision for your wedding day.

### Venue and Basic Amenities
- Venue: Access to the ceremony and reception spaces. This usually includes a specified number of hours for your event.
- Furniture: Tables, chairs, linens, and sometimes decorative items such as centerpieces.
- Setup and Cleanup: The staff will set up the ceremony and reception areas and clean up afterward, alleviating you and your guests of these responsibilities.

### Food and Beverage
- Catering: A variety of menu options ranging from buffet style to plated dinners, often with the ability to customize based on dietary needs.
- Beverages: Alcoholic and non-alcoholic drink options, which may include a cash bar, limited open bar, or fully open bar.

**Personnel**

- Staff: On-site staff for the event, including waitstaff, bartenders, and security.
- Wedding Coordinator: Day-of coordination services to ensure your wedding runs smoothly, with some packages offering more extensive planning services.

**Additional Inclusions**

- Accommodations: Some venues, particularly destination wedding locations, may include a night's stay for the newlyweds and sometimes offer room blocks for guests at a discounted rate.
- Entertainment: Basic DJ or live music services for the ceremony and reception.
- Photography: Limited photography services or partnerships with local photographers to capture your day (though many couples choose to hire their photographers for more comprehensive coverage).
- Cake: A wedding cake and sometimes a groom's cake, with options to customize design and flavors.
- Transportation: Shuttle service for guests, especially for venues that are remote or have limited parking.
- Extras: Many packages also offer special touches like a champagne toast, a bridal suite for getting ready, and various decor options.

**Things to Consider**

While all-inclusive packages cover a wide range of services, it's important to review the specifics of what each venue offers and any potential limitations. Some aspects, like floral arrangements, hair and makeup services, or customized decor, may require additional vendors. Moreover, while these packages offer convenience, ensure the options align with your personal preferences and wedding vision. Always inquire about customization options and additional costs to tailor the package to your needs.

Lastly, when considering an all-inclusive package, understand the payment structure, deposit requirements, and cancellation policy. Knowing these details upfront can help you budget more effectively and avoid any surprises down the line.

## 4.5   Package Levels, Add-ons, and Cost Considerations

All-inclusive destination wedding packages are tailored to fit a wide range of preferences and budgets, allowing couples to choose a package that best aligns with their vision and financial plans. Understanding the structure of package levels, the availability of add-ons, and the key cost considerations is crucial in making an informed decision. Here's a breakdown of how these packages are typically organized and what you might expect in terms of additional options and costs.

**Package Levels**

- **Basic or Essentials Package**:
  Designed for smaller gatherings or couples looking for simplicity, this level covers just the fundamental aspects of a wedding, such as the ceremony setup, officiant, a bouquet, a boutonniere, and sometimes a small reception or toast. It's ideal for elopements or intimate ceremonies.

- **Standard Package:**
  Building on the basics, the standard package includes additional features like a photographer, more

elaborate decor, a wider selection of menu options for the reception, and possibly some entertainment. This package is suited for couples expecting a moderate number of guests and desiring a balance between simplicity and customization.

- **Premium or Luxury Package:**
  For those seeking a comprehensive offering, the premium packages provide extensive options for customization, high-end decor, gourmet dining experiences, full entertainment choices, extended photography and videography services, and more elaborate floral arrangements. These packages may also offer exclusive venue choices and additional events, such as a welcome cocktail party or a day-after brunch.

## Add-ons and Customization Options

Add-ons allow couples to tailor their wedding package to their unique preferences, ensuring that every detail reflects their personal style and vision. Common add-ons include:

- Upgraded Decor and Floral Designs: Options for personalized themes, colors, and arrangements that go beyond the standard offerings.
- Gourmet Dining and Premium Beverages: Specialty menus, signature cocktails, and wine upgrades to enhance the culinary experience.
- Entertainment Enhancements: Live bands, cultural performances, or fireworks displays to create unforgettable moments.
- Beauty and Spa Services: Expanded options for hair, makeup, and spa treatments for the couple and their bridal party.

- Extended Photography/Videography: Additional hours of coverage, special shoots like a "trash the dress" session, or drone footage.
- Guest Experiences: Organized group excursions, special activities, or private transportation services for guests.

**Cost Considerations**

The cost of all-inclusive destination wedding packages can vary widely based on the destination, resort, package level, guest count, and chosen add-ons. Basic packages might start from a few thousand dollars for very intimate weddings, with prices increasing significantly for premium packages and as more personalized elements are added.

- Package Pricing: Always review what's included in the package price and understand any limitations or exclusions. Some packages offer significant value by bundling services at a lower cost than if sourced individually.
- Add-on Costs: Be mindful of the prices for optional add-ons, as these can quickly increase the overall cost of your wedding. Prioritize which elements are most important to you and allocate your budget accordingly.
- External Vendor Fees: Some venues charge extra fees if you choose to bring in outside vendors (e.g., photographers, makeup artists) not included in their preferred list.
- Travel and Accommodation: Consider the travel and accommodation costs for yourselves and potentially for key family members or bridal party members, depending on your arrangements.

**Final Thoughts**

When selecting an all-inclusive destination wedding package, it's essential to balance your desires with your budget, understanding that the base package cost is just the starting point. By carefully selecting add-ons and being mindful of additional expenses, you can create a beautifully personalized wedding that aligns with your financial considerations. Transparent communication with your venue or wedding planner about costs and options will help ensure that there are no surprises and that your wedding day is as magical and stress-free as envisioned.

# 4.6   Communicating with Your Resort Wedding Coordinator

Organizing a destination wedding at an all-inclusive resort requires clear and consistent communication with your resort wedding coordinator. This professional is your primary contact and guide, ensuring that every aspect of your wedding aligns with your vision while taking full advantage of the all-inclusive amenities and services. Here's a guide to effectively communicating and planning with your resort wedding coordinator.

**Initial Engagement**
- Introduction and Vision Sharing: Your journey starts with a detailed discussion about your wedding vision, preferences, and must-haves. This initial consultation is critical for setting the tone and direction of your wedding planning. Share your desired themes, colors, and overall atmosphere you wish to create, emphasizing any specific requests or ideas that are important to you.

- Setting Up Communication Channels: Agree on the most efficient communication channels for ongoing discussions. Most all-inclusive resorts are accustomed to working with international couples, offering flexible communication methods such as emails, scheduled calls, or virtual meetings to accommodate different time zones.

**Detailed Planning**
- Utilizing Resort Planning Tools: Leverage the resort's wedding planning tools and documents. These may include timelines, budget planners, and checklists tailored to the resort's specific offerings and services. Such resources help streamline the planning process and ensure comprehensive coverage of all details.

- Vendor and Service Coordination: Your resort wedding coordinator will facilitate all arrangements with onsite vendors included in your all-inclusive package, such as florists, caterers, photographers, and entertainers. Clearly communicate your preferences and desires for each service to allow your coordinator to effectively represent your interests.

- Incorporating Personalization: Work with your coordinator to add personal touches that reflect your relationship and enhance the guest experience. Discuss opportunities for customizing your ceremony and reception within the framework of the all-inclusive package, from menu selections to décor options.

**Navigating Logistics**

- Understanding Legalities: The coordinator will advise on the legal and logistical aspects of marrying at the destination, including documentation requirements and any necessary arrangements for a legally binding or symbolic ceremony.

- Scheduling Pre-Wedding Visits: If possible, arrange for a pre-wedding visit to meet with your coordinator and conduct site inspections, menu tastings, and final discussions about the wedding layout. If a visit isn't feasible, request virtual tours or photos to aid in decision-making.

**Final Preparations**
- Reviewing Final Details: Conduct a comprehensive review of the wedding timeline, confirming the schedule of events, vendor deliveries, and any special arrangements. This final check ensures all elements of your wedding align with your expectations.

- Emergency Plans: Exchange emergency contact information and establish a day-of communication plan with your coordinator. Knowing how to quickly address any last-minute adjustments or issues will provide peace of mind.

# Chapter 5
# The Guest List and Invitations

Congratulations, you've set the date and found the perfect venue for your destination wedding! Now, it's time to think about who you'll share this special day with and how you'll invite them. Crafting your guest list and sending out invitations for a destination wedding isn't just about announcing the details; it's about creating excitement and giving your loved ones a glimpse into the adventure that awaits. Let's navigate the process of curating your guest list and designing invitations that set the tone for your unforgettable celebration.

## 5.1    Building Your Guest List: Starting with Deciding Guest Size

Embarking on the journey of a destination wedding starts with a pivotal decision that shapes much of the planning process: determining the size of your guest list. This isn't just about numbers; it's about envisioning the atmosphere and intimacy of your celebration, and balancing dreams with practicality. Here's how to navigate the delicate balance of deciding on your guest list size for a destination wedding.

### Consider the Venue Capacity:
Start with the logistics—how many people can your venue comfortably accommodate? This number can help you narrow down your list.

### Prioritize Intimacy:
Think about who truly matters to you and your partner. A destination wedding is an opportunity for meaningful interactions. Start with your inner circle—family and closest

friends whom you can't imagine not being part of your day. Then, create subsequent circles of friends, colleagues, and acquaintances. This approach helps you prioritize invitations based on your relationships and the overall feel you want for your wedding.

### Be Mindful of Guests' Travel Capabilities

Remember, not everyone may be able to afford the trip or be able to travel due to health, work, or family reasons. The location you choose may influence who can realistically attend. Distant or remote destinations might be challenging for older relatives or friends with limited travel budgets. Consider the willingness and ability of your loved ones to travel as you decide on your guest list size.

### Plus-Ones and Family Dynamics

Decide early on your policy for plus-ones and children, as this can significantly affect your guest count. While including everyone's partners and families might be ideal, it may not be feasible for a destination wedding. Be clear and consistent in your approach to avoid misunderstandings.

### Flexibility and Adjustments

As you plan, you may need to adjust your guest list size. Keep an open mind and maintain open communication with your partner about what changes might be necessary, whether due to budget adjustments, venue constraints, or guest RSVPs.

## 5.2    Crafting the Invitations

Your wedding invitations are not just a formality—they're the prologue to your love story's next chapter, set in a breathtaking locale far from home. They set the tone for your destination wedding, offering guests a glimpse into the adventure that awaits. Here's how to craft invitations that not only inform but also enchant and excite your guests.

### The First Glimpse into Your Adventure:

Your wedding invitations are more than just paper; they're the first taste of your wedding's vibe and an exciting reveal of your destination. Here's how to make them count:

- Start with Save-the-Dates: For destination weddings, sending out save-the-dates is crucial, and the earlier, the better. Aim for 8-12 months in advance, giving your guests ample time to plan, save, and take leave from work.

- Incorporate Your Destination's Flair: Let your destination inspire your invitation design. Whether it's tropical motifs for a beach wedding or elegant scripts for a European château, your invites should echo the essence of your location.

- The Narrative: The wording of your invitation is just as important as its design. It should not only provide essential information but also convey the tone of your wedding. Whether you opt for traditional, formal wording or something more personal and whimsical, ensure it reflects your personality as a couple and the spirit of your celebration.

- Provide Essential Information: Beyond the basics (who, what, when, where), include details specific to a destination wedding, like travel tips, accommodation options, and a brief itinerary of events. Consider creating a wedding website for more detailed information. This can be a comprehensive resource for guests, containing updates, additional details about the destination, a more detailed itinerary, RSVP functionality, and even a Q&A section. Think about potential questions your guests might have—from travel tips and currency exchange rates to local customs and what to pack—and provide detailed answers. Make sure the website address or QR code is clearly included in your invitation suite.

- Consider the Formality: Your invitation should reflect the formality of your event. A laid-back beach wedding might call for lighter, more playful invitations, while a grand ballroom affair suits a more formal approach.

**RSVPs and Communication**

In the world of destination weddings, managing RSVPs and maintaining clear communication with your guests transform from simple tasks into crucial elements of your planning process. Given the extra effort and expense for guests to travel, ensuring a seamless flow of information and understanding their attendance plans become paramount. Let's explore how to handle RSVPs and communication with grace and efficiency, making sure your guests feel informed, welcomed, and excited about the journey ahead.

- Navigating Confirmations and Queries: Managing RSVPs for a destination wedding requires a bit more patience and flexibility. Set an RSVP deadline early enough to adjust bookings as needed but allow for some leeway as guests work out their travel plans.

- Make Use of Technology: A wedding website can be invaluable for managing RSVPs and keeping guests informed of any changes or additional details. It's also a great platform for guests to ask questions and for you to provide travel advice and recommendations.

- Personal Touch: For those not as tech-savvy, ensure you have a way to communicate directly, whether through phone calls, text messages, or even traditional mail. Keeping an open line of communication is key to ensuring everyone feels included and prepared.

## After the RSVP Deadline

- Final Confirmations: Once you have a final headcount, confirm details with your vendors, adjust accommodations and transportation arrangements as necessary, and finalize seating charts and event itineraries.

- A Word of Thanks: After your RSVP deadline and leading up to the wedding, consider sending a thank-you message to those who have confirmed. This can express your excitement about sharing the experience with them and set a positive tone for the upcoming celebration.

## Handling Delicate Situations

All Aboard with Grace: It's possible that some guests might feel left out or unable to attend due to the destination aspect. Handle these situations with understanding and empathy. When possible, have a personal conversation (or send a thoughtful message) to them. Offer to celebrate with them in another way, such as a casual get-together before or after the wedding.

Travel costs can prohibit some guests from attending your destination wedding, which can be disappointing for both you and them. Acknowledge their situation with understanding and compassion. Let them know you understand their constraints and that their presence will be missed but not expected.

You may explore ways to include them in the celebration virtually. Live-streaming the ceremony or sharing a video call during key moments allows them to be part of your day, even from afar.

# Chapter 6
# Vendors and Coordination

Embarking on the adventure of a destination wedding brings its own set of challenges and rewards, particularly when it comes to selecting and coordinating with vendors from afar. Your wedding vendors are the magicians behind the scenes, turning your dream into reality. From florists to photographers, caterers to musicians, each plays a pivotal role in crafting the atmosphere and experience of your big day. In this chapter, we'll navigate the waters of selecting and working with vendors for your destination wedding, ensuring a seamless and stress-free coordination.

## 6.1   Hiring a Wedding Planner: Pros and Cons

When it comes to planning a destination wedding, the decision to hire a wedding planner can significantly impact your planning process and the overall experience of your big day. A wedding planner specializes in the logistics and design of weddings, offering professional advice, vendor recommendations, and day-of coordination services. For a destination wedding, where the logistics can be more complex due to the location, a wedding planner can be especially valuable. However, there are both advantages and disadvantages to consider.

**Pros of Hiring a Wedding Planner**

- Expertise and Experience: Wedding planners bring a wealth of knowledge and experience, navigating wedding planning challenges with ease. They're familiar with the best practices, potential pitfalls, and have a network of reliable vendors.

- Local Insight: If you're marrying in a location you're unfamiliar with, a local wedding planner provides invaluable insight into the area. They can suggest the best venues and local vendors, understanding the nuances of the location, from weather patterns to legal requirements.

- Stress Reduction: Planning a wedding can be stressful, especially from afar. A wedding planner takes on the bulk of the planning stress, handling everything from vendor coordination to scheduling, allowing you to enjoy the lead-up to your wedding.

- Time-Saving: A wedding planner can save you countless hours by researching vendors, managing contracts, and organizing logistics. This is especially beneficial for couples with demanding jobs or limited free time.

- Budget Management: Experienced planners can help manage your wedding budget, ensuring you get the best value for your money. They can negotiate with vendors on your behalf and help you avoid costly mistakes.

- Cultural Navigator: For weddings in a foreign country, planners can bridge cultural differences, ensuring that your wedding respects local traditions and practices while still honoring your vision.

**Cons of Hiring a Wedding Planner**

- Additional Cost: Hiring a wedding planner is an additional expense. Depending on their level of involvement, this can range from a few thousand dollars to a significant portion of your wedding budget.

- Less Hands-On Experience: Some couples enjoy the process of planning every detail of their wedding. Hiring a planner might result in feeling less involved in the decision-making process.

- Finding the Right Match: Not every planner might align with your style, vision, or personality. It can take time and research to find a planner you feel comfortable with and trust to execute your vision.

- Potential for Overdependence: Relying too heavily on a planner might mean missing out on personal touches you could have contributed to the wedding. It's important to maintain a balance between delegation and personal involvement.

- Risk of Miscommunication: Working with a planner requires clear communication. Misunderstandings can arise, especially if you're not clear about your expectations or if the planner doesn't fully grasp your vision.

## 6.2    Selecting Local vs. International Vendors

There's a certain charm and authenticity in sourcing local vendors who can bring a taste of the destination to your wedding. However, for certain services, you might prefer vendors from home whom you trust and have a rapport with.

- Local Vendors: Often more cost-effective; bring local knowledge and flavor; however, might present language barriers or different business practices.

- International Vendors: Might align more closely with your expectations; easier communication; but could significantly increase costs due to travel and accommodation requirements.

## 6.3    Coordinating with Vendors from Afar

Organizing a destination wedding means managing vendors from a distance, which can be a complex task fraught with challenges. However, with the right approach and tools, you can ensure effective coordination, turning potential obstacles into manageable tasks. Here's how to effectively work with vendors for your destination wedding, no matter the miles between you.

### Establishing Clear Communication Channels

- Direct and Regular Contact: Set up regular check-ins with your vendors through video calls, emails, or phone calls. Establishing a routine for updates and discussions helps keep everyone aligned and allows for timely adjustments to plans.

- Language Considerations: If working in a non-native language, consider hiring a bilingual wedding planner or a translator to ensure clear communication. Misunderstandings in contracts or discussions about expectations can lead to significant issues down the line.

**Utilizing Technology**

- Digital Planning Tools: Leverage technology to share ideas, documents, and updates. Platforms like Google Drive, Trello, and wedding planning apps allow you to organize contracts, inspiration boards, and schedules in one accessible place.

- Virtual Site Visits: If you can't visit the venue or meet with vendors in person, ask for virtual tours or meetings on-site. Many vendors are equipped to provide virtual consultations, which can give you a better feel for their services and how they align with your vision.

**Building a Trusted Team on the Ground**

- Local Wedding Planner: A local planner or coordinator can be your eyes and ears on the ground. They can oversee vendor activities, conduct site visits on your behalf, and provide valuable insights into local customs and vendor reputations.

- Vendor References: Before finalizing any contracts, request references and review portfolios of previous weddings. Speak directly with past clients if possible, to get a sense of their experience working with the vendor from afar.

## Managing Contracts and Payments

- Detailed Contracts: Ensure every detail is covered in your contracts, from delivery times and services provided to cancellation policies and payment schedules. Having everything in writing protects both parties and sets clear expectations.

- Secure Payment Methods: Use secure, traceable payment methods for transactions. Be aware of currency exchange rates and international transaction fees. Tools like PayPal or international bank transfers are commonly used, offering both security and convenience.

## Conducting a Pre-Wedding Visit

- Site Inspection: If possible, plan a trip to your wedding location a few months before the event. Meeting vendors in person, tasting the menu, and seeing the venue can provide reassurance and allow for last-minute adjustments.

- Trial Runs: Use this visit to schedule trials (e.g., hair and makeup, menu tasting) and finalize details like decor, seating arrangements, and flow of the day with your vendors.

### Preparing for the Unexpected

- Plan B: Discuss backup plans with your vendors for unforeseen circumstances, such as inclement weather or delays. Knowing there's a flexible plan in place can reduce stress and ensure a smooth celebration.

- Emergency Contacts: Have a list of all vendor contacts readily available, and ensure they have the contacts of your wedding planner or designated coordinator. Quick communication can resolve issues before they escalate..

## 6.4   Navigating Contracts and Payments

Understanding and negotiating contracts with vendors is critical. Pay attention to cancellation policies, payment schedules, and any clauses that could affect your wedding plans.

- Legal Review: Consider having contracts reviewed by a legal professional, especially for significant expenses.
- Payment Methods: Understand the preferred payment methods for each vendor and any potential international transaction fees.
- Utilizing Technology: Use digital platforms for sharing documents and information, allowing for real-time collaboration and updates.

# Chapter 7
# The Ceremony and Reception

The heart of your destination wedding lies in the ceremony and reception — the moments where promises are made, and celebrations unfold under foreign skies or amidst unfamiliar landscapes, yet everything feels perfectly at home because you're surrounded by your loved ones. Crafting these pivotal parts of your wedding day requires attention to detail, a deep understanding of the locale's offerings, and a personal touch that speaks to your journey as a couple. Here's how to ensure your ceremony and reception are as seamless as they are memorable.

## 7.1    Planning the Ceremony

Planning the ceremony is a central part of organizing your destination wedding, blending the logistical needs of your chosen locale with the personal touches that make the day uniquely yours.

Begin by carefully selecting your setting. The venue should resonate with your desired theme and ambiance, be it a serene beach, lush garden, historic estate, or picturesque vineyard. It's beneficial to choose a venue experienced in hosting destination weddings, capable of accommodating your specific needs. If possible, a preliminary visit (even by virtual) to the venue is advisable to understand the space better, visualize the event, and discuss crucial details with either the venue coordinator or your wedding planner. This visit is also an opportune time to explore locations for the ceremony, reception, and photo sessions.

Understanding the local legal and cultural landscape is also important. Research the destination's legal requirements for marriage, which may include specific residency conditions, applications for marriage licenses, and necessary documents. Additionally, acquainting yourself with and respecting local customs can enrich your ceremony and show respect for the culture hosting your special day.

Decide on the structure and format of your ceremony, taking into account any cultural or religious traditions you wish to incorporate. Whether you opt for a traditional ceremony with time-honored rituals or a more modern and personalized approach, make sure it reflects your values and beliefs.

When it comes to the finer details of your ceremony, decision-making extends to selecting an officiant who either travels with you or is locally based but legally recognized to conduct your ceremony. Whether it's a religious leader, a close friend or family member, or a professional officiant, ensure that they understand your wishes and are able to convey them eloquently.

Personalizing your vows, incorporating meaningful readings, or including special rituals can deepen the ceremony's emotional impact. Music selection and sound logistics are equally important, especially in outdoor or unconventional venues, ensuring the ambiance complements your ceremony's mood and all verbal exchanges are heard clearly.

Communicating detailed information to your guests is crucial. A comprehensive itinerary that outlines the ceremony time, location, and transportation logistics, possibly conveyed through a welcome packet or a dedicated wedding website, will keep everyone informed. Clarity about the dress code, considering the venue's style and local weather, will also help guests prepare adequately.

Lastly, a rehearsal with your wedding party, officiant, and involved family members is critical for ironing out the logistics of timing, positioning, and roles. Having a day-of coordinator, whether a professional or a trusted friend, to oversee ceremony logistics can alleviate stress and enable you to immerse fully in the joy and significance of your union.

While meticulous planning is key, readiness to embrace the unexpected allows you to cherish the moment, regardless of any deviations from the plan. The essence of your destination wedding ceremony lies in celebrating your love and commitment, with each decision reflecting your collective values and dreams for the future.

## 7.2    Designing the Ceremony Format and Order of Program

Your destination wedding ceremony is a chance to weave your love story into a beautiful and meaningful experience. But with stunning backdrops and cultural variations, how do you design a ceremony format that's both personal and unforgettable? This section guides you through crafting the perfect order of program for your destination wedding.

### Embrace the Flexibility

Destination weddings often allow for more flexibility compared to traditional ceremonies. Here's what sets them apart:

- Intimate Gatherings: Destination weddings typically have smaller guest lists, creating a more intimate atmosphere. This allows for a more personalized ceremony that reflects your unique bond.

- Cultural Inspiration: Embrace the local customs and traditions of your chosen location. Weaving in elements that resonate with you can add a touch of cultural flair to your ceremony.

**Crafting the Ceremony Flow**

While there's room for creativity, a well-structured ceremony order ensures a smooth and meaningful flow. Here's a typical outline to consider, with opportunities for personalization:

1) **Prelude**:
   As guests arrive, set the mood with calming music that complements your chosen location.
2) **Processional**:
   This is the formal entrance of the wedding party, often starting with the groom, followed by the bridesmaids, groomsmen, and finally, the bride escorted by a loved one.
3) **Welcome and Introduction**:
   The officiant will greet the guests and share a few words about the couple and the significance of the ceremony.
4) **Opening Remarks**:
   This is where you can incorporate a short reading, poem, or personal anecdote that sets the tone for the ceremony. Consider incorporating a local tradition or language element here if it resonates with you.
5) **Exchange of Vows**:
   The heart of the ceremony, this is where you express your love and commitment to each other. You can choose to write your own vows or use traditional options.
6) **Ring Exchange**:
   A simple yet symbolic act of solidifying your bond.

7) **Unity Ceremony (Optional)**:
   This symbolic ritual represents the joining of two lives. Popular options include lighting a unity candle, planting a unity tree, or blending sands of different colors.
8) **Pronouncement of Marriage**:
   The officiant declares you husband and wife.
9) **Presentation of the Couple**:
   The officiant introduces you as a married couple for the first time.
10) **Recessional**:
   Exit the ceremony space together as newlyweds, often to celebratory music.

**Personalization is Key**

This is just a framework, and the beauty of a destination wedding lies in its ability to be personalized. Here are some ways to make your ceremony truly your own:

- Readings: Select readings that resonate with your love story or cultural background. Ask a loved one to perform a reading in their native language for a special touch.
- Music: Choose music that reflects your personalities and the overall mood of your ceremony. Consider incorporating local musicians or instruments for a unique touch.
- Rituals: Think beyond the traditional unity ceremony. Explore cultural rituals or traditions that hold significance for you and your partner.

**Considerations for Your Guests**

- Program Handouts: Provide guests with program handouts or fans that outline the ceremony order. This can include translations if incorporating elements in a foreign language, making the ceremony inclusive and accessible to all guests.

- Briefing Your Wedding Party: Ensure your wedding party is familiar with the ceremony format and their roles. A rehearsal or detailed briefing can help prevent any confusion and ensure everyone feels comfortable with the proceedings.
- Timing and Comfort: Consider the comfort of your guests, especially in outdoor or unusual settings. Plan for shade, hydration, or even seat cushions if the ceremony is lengthy or the climate is extreme.

**Tips for a Flawless Ceremony**
- Communicate with your Officiant: Discuss your vision for the ceremony and any cultural elements you wish to incorporate.
- Rehearsal Makes Perfect: Schedule a rehearsal, even if it's informal, to ensure the ceremony flows smoothly on the big day.
- Embrace the Moment: Relax, soak in the love surrounding you, and enjoy this once-in-a-lifetime experience!

# 7.3   Planning the Reception

Planning the reception in a far-flung locale presents its own set of challenges and opportunities, but with careful consideration and a bit of creativity, you can create an unforgettable experience for everyone involved.

**Choosing the Reception Venue**
When you begin to plan your reception, the first step is selecting the right venue. The venue should not only captivate the beauty and essence of the destination but also

accommodate your guest list comfortably and meet your logistical needs. Many couples opt for the same venue for both ceremony and reception for convenience and cost-efficiency, but exploring nearby options can unveil hidden gems that might better suit your vision.

### Decor and Lighting

Once the venue is secured, crafting the ambiance through decor and lighting is your next focus. The beauty of a destination wedding is in its setting, which can often require minimal enhancement to shine. However, personalized details—such as table settings that incorporate local flora or lighting that mirrors the hues of the sunset—can transform a space into a reflection of your personal style and story.

### Culinary Experience

The culinary experience is a cornerstone of any wedding reception, and a destination wedding offers a unique opportunity to showcase the local cuisine. Work with your venue or caterer to design a menu that highlights local ingredients and dishes, offering your guests an authentic taste of the region. Whether it's a formal seated dinner, a relaxed buffet, or themed food stations, the key is to balance quality and variety while catering to dietary preferences and restrictions.

### Entertainment and music

Entertainment and music play a pivotal role in setting the tone for the evening. Hiring local musicians or bands not only supports the local community but also imbues your reception with a sense of place. Alternatively, a DJ can offer a more varied playlist that caters to all tastes. Remember to consider the acoustics of your venue and any noise restrictions that may be in place.

## Seating Arrangements

As you plan, keep your guests' comfort and experience at the forefront. This includes thoughtful seating arrangements, ensuring ample space for mingling and dancing, and providing for their needs—be it through climate-appropriate amenities, transportation to and from the venue, or guidance on local customs and languages.

The art of seating arrangements is in creating an environment that encourages conversation, celebration, and a sense of community among your guests. In a destination setting, where guests may have traveled from far and wide, fostering an atmosphere of intimacy and connection becomes even more crucial. Consider the relationships and dynamics between different groups of guests when planning your seating chart. Mixing friends and family members from different circles can spark new friendships, but it's also important to ensure that everyone has at least a few familiar faces at their table.

For receptions held outdoors or in large, open spaces, consider the layout carefully to promote a flow that feels both welcoming and intimate. Utilize the natural features of your venue to create distinct areas for dining, dancing, and lounging, allowing guests to move seamlessly through the space. Round tables are traditionally popular for fostering conversation, but don't shy away from mixing table shapes and sizes for a more dynamic setup. Additionally, personalized touches like place cards or small favors at each seat can make your guests feel valued and included in your special day.

For outdoor celebrations, you need to have a clear plan for inclement weather. Whether it's providing parasols for shade or having a beautiful indoor backup venue, being prepared will ensure your celebration goes smoothly regardless of the skies.

**Logistics and Flow**

Don't forget the logistics of timing and flow. A well-structured timeline that allows for the natural progression of the evening—from cocktail hour to dinner, speeches, and dancing—ensures a seamless experience for guests and vendors alike. Coordination with your wedding planner or day-of coordinator is essential to manage the schedule and handle any unforeseen issues.

**Infusing Local Flavor**

Incorporating local traditions or elements into your reception can add a layer of depth and meaning to your celebration. Whether it's a traditional dance, a customary toast, or a local custom, these touches invite your guests to fully immerse themselves in the cultural experience of your destination.

**Shared Joy and Gratitude**

Finally, remember that the reception is a celebration of your new beginning together. While the details are important, the heart of the reception lies in the joy, love, and community that surround you. Embrace the unique backdrop of your destination, let your personalities shine through in the details, and above all, ensure that the night is a reflection of your shared joy and gratitude for those who have come to celebrate with you.

By addressing these key elements with attention and care, your destination wedding reception will not only celebrate your union but also create lasting memories for you and your guests, capturing the essence of the destination and the magic of the moment.

## 7.4   Memorable Menus and Music

The reception menu and music are pivotal in setting the tone for your destination wedding celebration. They have the power to transport your guests through flavors and rhythms, making your wedding not just an event but an unforgettable experience.

All-inclusive resorts typically offer a selection of pre-designed menus for weddings. These menus provide a solid foundation, but there's often room for customization within certain parameters.

### Curating a Memorable Menu

The journey begins with a menu that mirrors the rich palette of the destination's cuisine, inviting your guests on a gastronomic adventure that captures the spirit of the locale. Collaborating with your wedding coordinator or caterer, you can select dishes that spotlight regional flavors and ingredients, transforming each meal into a story of discovery. Interactive elements, such as live cooking stations or food demonstrations, add a dynamic layer to the dining experience, offering a glimpse into local culinary traditions while entertaining your guests.

In addition, ensure there are options for guests with dietary restrictions, allergies, or preferences. A thoughtful menu accommodates everyone, making each guest feel valued and taken care of.

### Additional Tips

Opting for menu options that capitalize on fresh and seasonal ingredients is key to ensuring the food at your reception is both delicious and memorable. Seasonal produce not only tastes better but also adds an authentic touch to your menu, reflecting the local environment and its offerings.

The visual presentation of your food plays a significant role in the overall dining experience. Work closely with the catering team to design table settings and choose garnishes that complement the aesthetic of your wedding. Creative plating techniques and thoughtful presentation can transform even the simplest dishes into culinary masterpieces, making each course a visual delight that anticipates the flavors to come.

No wedding reception is complete without a dessert that leaves a lasting impression. Whether you opt for a traditional wedding cake, an assortment of gourmet pastries, or a local dessert that ties into the destination's culinary culture, make sure it's something that satisfies the sweet tooth and adds an element of celebration.

## Setting the Tone with Music

Music harmonizes with your destination, accentuating its ambiance and setting a backdrop that complements its natural beauty or historical charm. The choice of music, be it a local ensemble echoing traditional melodies, a DJ blending beats under the stars of a beach venue, or a classical quartet within the walls of an ancient estate, becomes the soundtrack of your celebration, elevating the atmosphere and enriching the sense of place.

The musical journey extends from the ceremony to the dance floor, with each selection encapsulating a chapter of your love story. Live musicians can bestow a personalized and elegant aura to your vows, while the first dance—a pinnacle moment—should be accompanied by a song that holds profound meaning to you both, heralding the night's festivities. Collaborative playlist creation with your musicians ensures the evening pulses with energy, inviting every guest to partake in the joy and celebration.

Special performances, whether they're dances that nod to your cultural heritage or unexpected musical acts that reflect a shared passion, serve as delightful interludes that surprise and engage your guests. These performances deepen the connection, bringing layers of personal and cultural narratives to the forefront, making your wedding not just an event, but a heartfelt celebration of your union.

## 7.5   Ensuring Guest Comfort

Ensuring the comfort of your guests at a destination wedding is crucial, given the effort they make to join your celebration. The essence of guest comfort lies in making them feel appreciated and integral to the festivities from start to finish, which requires thoughtful planning and attention to detail.

### Accommodations and Transportation

Providing a range of lodging options near the wedding venue allows guests to choose accommodations that suit their budget and preferences. Securing a block of rooms can help ensure availability and may offer guests the convenience of group rates. Equally important is arranging transportation to and from wedding events, which can alleviate the stress of navigating unfamiliar areas, ensuring safe and easy travel for your guests.

### Climate Considerations

The climate of your wedding destination plays a crucial role in guest comfort. For warmer locales, offering amenities like fans or parasols can help keep guests cool, while in cooler climates, providing blankets or outdoor heaters can add a layer of warmth to outdoor activities. Informing guests about the expected weather and suggesting appropriate attire through your invitations or wedding website allows them to come prepared, enhancing their overall comfort.

**Thoughtful Amenities**

Welcome bags tailored to the destination and filled with useful items such as local snacks, water, and sunscreen offer a warm reception and demonstrate thoughtfulness. Providing comfortable seating and rest areas throughout the venue ensures guests can relax and enjoy the celebration, particularly important during events that span several days.

**Dietary and Health Needs**

Accommodating dietary preferences is essential to ensure all guests can partake in the dining experience. Ensuring the venue is accessible for guests with mobility issues and preparing for medical needs underscores the importance of guest welfare and comfort at your celebration.

**Engaging and Inclusive Activities**

Offering a variety of activities allows guests to choose their preferred level of engagement based on their interests. Quiet spaces designated for relaxation or conversation cater to those who might need a break from the main festivities, ensuring everyone's comfort.

**Clear Communication**

Providing detailed information about the wedding events, including schedules, dress codes, and logistics, helps guests plan their participation. This can be achieved through a dedicated wedding website, welcome bags, or direct communication, ensuring guests are well-informed and comfortable.

**Special Touches**

Personal acknowledgments, such as handwritten notes or direct greetings, can make guests feel truly valued for their presence. Sending off guests with a farewell token or hosting a breakfast gathering the day after the wedding offers a warm conclusion to the celebration and expresses gratitude.

# Chapter 8
# Photography and Videography

One of the perks of an all-inclusive package is the convenience of having many services bundled together. Hiring the resort's team eliminates the stress of finding vendors from afar. They'll be familiar with the venue and have experience capturing weddings at the location, knowing the best lighting and angles to utilize. This can be a major advantage, especially if your chosen destination is particularly scenic or has unique logistical considerations.

While seemingly convenient, in-house services might not always be the most cost-effective option. Be sure to compare the quality and inclusions of the resort's photography/videography packages with hiring an independent photographer and videographer. Factor in the number of hours of coverage, the number of photographers/videographers included, and the final deliverables (edited photos, raw footage, albums, etc.).

If you decide to hire an external photographer and videographer, it's essential to choose professionals whose style matches your vision and who have experience in capturing the nuances of destination weddings. Their ability to document the beauty of the location, the emotions of the day, and the joyous celebration will allow you to relive your special day for years to come.

## 8.1    Selecting the Right Professionals

When selecting your photography and videography team, begin by exploring their portfolios to ensure their artistic style aligns with your expectations.

### Evaluating Their Experience and Expertise

Professionals with experience in destination weddings bring an understanding of the unique challenges and opportunities these settings present, such as diverse lighting conditions and capturing the locale's beauty. Inquire about their experience with weddings similar to yours in size, style, and location. If they've worked at your chosen destination or venue before, ask to see examples. Speaking to past clients can offer insights into their professionalism and the satisfaction with the final product.

### Assessing Compatibility

Your comfort with the photographer or videographer is essential, as they'll be with you during intimate and emotional moments. During initial consultations, assess whether you feel understood and at ease with them. It's important that they share your vision for the wedding and are enthusiastic about capturing it in a way that aligns with your expectations.

### Discussing Logistics and Details

Discuss package details thoroughly to understand what's included, such as the number of photographers/videographers, hours of coverage, and expected deliverables like albums, digital files, and highlight reels. Ask about their contingency plans for unexpected situations like equipment failure or personal illness, ensuring they have clear strategies in place.

### Finalizing Your Choice

If possible, arrange for a pre-wedding site visit, especially if they haven't worked at your venue before. Since in-person visits are not feasible in most destination weddings, consider requesting a virtual site visit. Many sites are now offering virtual tours or can provide drone footage and photographs of the venue, which can be a valuable tool for planning your photography and videography needs remotely. This virtual option can still allow them to familiarize themselves with the venue layout, lighting conditions, and potential photo and video locations, ensuring they can capture your wedding day as effectively as if they had visited in person.

When finalizing your choice, review contracts carefully, ensuring they outline all services, deliverables, payment schedules, cancellation policies, and copyright arrangements clearly. While cost is a consideration, remember that photography and videography are investments in preserving your wedding memories. Balance budget considerations with the importance of quality and compatibility, choosing a professional who will capture your day in a way that allows you to relive it for years to come.

## 8.2 Effective Communication and Planning

Maintaining open and clear lines of communication with your photography and videography team is essential, especially when dealing with geographical distances. Setting up a schedule for regular updates through video calls or emails will keep everyone on the same page. For instances where language barriers exist, consider the help of a fluent intermediary or translation services to ensure that every detail is communicated clearly, avoiding any potential misunderstandings.

### Sharing Your Vision and Expectations

It's vital to share your vision and expectations clearly with your photography and videography team. Using vision boards or inspiration galleries can effectively convey the style, mood, and specific shots you're aiming for. Platforms like Pinterest are great tools for this purpose. Providing detailed briefs will also help outline your expectations more clearly, including key moments you want captured, specific locations for shots, and any unique elements of your wedding that should be highlighted.

### Developing a Comprehensive Itinerary

Providing a detailed itinerary of the wedding events, complete with timings and locations for each segment of the celebration, is crucial. This enables your photography and videography team to plan their positioning and equipment setup to capture key moments flawlessly. If feasible, a pre-wedding venue visit or a virtual tour should be arranged to scout locations, plan shots, and identify potential challenges together.

### Discussing the Shot List and Must-Have Moments

Creating a shot list is an important step in ensuring that no critical moments or individuals are missed. While trusting the professional's creativity and discretion is important, highlighting "must-have" shots or moments prioritizes your most valued memories. This approach ensures that photographers and videographers allocate appropriate time and resources to capture these essential elements.

### Planning for the Unexpected

Contingency planning for unforeseen circumstances, such as adverse weather conditions or lighting challenges, is a necessary part of the planning process. Discussing these contingency plans in advance can alleviate stress and guarantee a smooth execution on your special day. Exchanging emergency contact information is also key to facilitating quick communication for any immediate decisions or adjustments needed on the wedding day.

## Confirming Details and Execution

A final review meeting close to the wedding date to go over the itinerary, shot list, and any last-minute details or adjustments is imperative. It's also crucial to have a clear understanding and written confirmation of the services to be provided. When finalizing arrangements, make sure your contracts are detailed, covering the scope of work, delivery timelines, copyright details, and the format in which the images and videos will be delivered. Understanding the inclusions of your package, from the number of hours of coverage to the type of post-production work, ensures that there are no surprises and that your wedding is documented beautifully and comprehensively.

# Chapter 9
# Attire and Beauty

## 9.1    Selecting Appropriate Attire for Your Destination

Selecting the perfect attire and ensuring your beauty shines through on your destination wedding day involves a delicate balance between your personal style, the local climate, and the wedding's overall theme. From flowing gowns that catch the sea breeze to lightweight suits that keep you cool under the sun, and beauty looks that withstand the elements, here's how to navigate attire and beauty for your destination wedding.

### Consider the Climate

When choosing your wedding attire for a destination event, the climate plays a crucial role in ensuring comfort and elegance. For warmer or tropical locales, lightweight and breathable fabrics like chiffon, linen, or silk are ideal to keep cool. Brides might gravitate towards flowy dresses with loose silhouettes for ease and comfort, while grooms can maintain a sharp look with linen suits or smart casual outfits suited to the beachy atmosphere. Conversely, weddings in cooler climates call for layers. Brides can add warmth and style with long sleeves, capes, or shawls, and grooms can opt for suits made of heavier fabrics such as velvet or brocade, offering both luxury and warmth.

### Respect Local Culture and Customs

It's important to show respect for the local culture and customs of your wedding destination, especially in places with strong cultural traditions. This may include dressing modestly or avoiding certain colors. Incorporating elements of the local culture into your wedding attire, such as accessories, colors, or patterns, can add a deeply personal touch to your celebration, honoring the setting in a meaningful way.

### Adapt to the Venue

The formality and physical setting of your venue should guide your attire choices. Formal settings like grand castles or historic villas might necessitate more formal attire, whereas a beach or garden wedding would be more suited to relaxed, romantic styles. Additionally, consider the venue's terrain when selecting your outfit and footwear. For outdoor settings, a dress that's easy to move in and appropriate footwear like flats, wedges, or stylish sandals can help navigate sandy or uneven grounds gracefully.

### Personal Comfort and Style

While it's essential to consider the destination, climate, and venue, your personal style and comfort should remain a priority. Choose wedding attire that reflects your personality and makes you feel confident and beautiful. Comfort is also key, as you will be in your wedding attire for an extended period, potentially facing varying temperatures and engaging in different activities.

### Coordinating with Your Wedding Party

When coordinating your wedding party's attire, consider the destination's climate and the venue's style. Providing a color palette or fabric suggestions can help achieve a cohesive look while allowing each member to choose outfits that reflect their personal style and ensure their comfort. Encouraging adaptability in their attire selections will not only align with the wedding's aesthetic but also contribute to a comfortable and enjoyable experience for everyone involved.

## 9.2    Beauty Considerations

Planning your beauty regimen for a destination wedding requires careful consideration of several factors including climate, location, and local cultural norms. These elements significantly influence your makeup, hair, and skincare choices, ensuring that you look and feel your best while fitting seamlessly into the unique ambiance of your chosen locale.

### Climate-Adaptive Makeup and Hair

Choosing weather-proof makeup and hairstyles that can withstand the destination's climate is essential. For humid destinations, opt for long-lasting, waterproof makeup products and oil-free formulas to prevent shine, complemented by setting sprays to maintain your look. In dryer climates, focus on using moisturizing products to keep your skin radiant. Select a hairstyle that not only complements the setting but also remains intact against local weather conditions. Updos or secured styles are ideal for windy settings, while embracing natural hair textures can work well in humid conditions to avoid frizz.

### Hiring Local Beauty Professionals

Utilizing the expertise of local beauty professionals can provide valuable insights into managing the local climate's effects on your hair and skin. They can recommend products and styles that ensure your beauty look remains flawless throughout your wedding day. If feasible, arrange trial sessions to test and refine your look based on local conditions, allowing for adjustments as needed.

**Pre-Wedding Skincare**

Tailor your skincare regimen in the weeks leading up to the wedding to suit the destination's climate. This may involve incorporating more hydrating products for dry locations or opting for lightweight, non-comedogenic items in humid environments. Sun protection is crucial, regardless of the destination, so include a high SPF sunscreen in your skincare routine to guard against sun damage, particularly if your wedding involves outdoor activities.

**Cultural and Location Considerations**

It's important to understand and respect the beauty standards and expectations of your wedding location, as these can influence your beauty choices. You might also consider adding local elements to your beauty look, such as using a flower native to the region in your hair or adopting a makeup palette inspired by the local scenery, adding a personal and location-specific touch to your appearance.

**Practical Beauty Logistics**

When preparing your beauty products for travel, opt for travel-sized and multi-purpose items to simplify your packing. Make sure your products comply with airline regulations, and consider how pressure changes during flights might affect liquids. An emergency beauty kit for the wedding day should include items for quick touch-ups, such as blotting papers, powder, lipstick, hair pins, and mini hairspray. Having a bridesmaid or a close friend keep this kit handy will ensure you can easily address any beauty mishaps.

## 9.3  Hair and Makeup Service in All-Inclusive Resorts

In all-inclusive destination wedding packages, hair and beauty care services are not typically included as standard features. While these packages usually cover the essentials like venue, catering, and decorations, hair and beauty care often fall into the category of additional services that can be added on for an extra fee.

However, many all-inclusive resorts and venues offer these services on-site or have partnerships with local salons and professionals. Couples can usually arrange for hair styling, makeup, and other beauty treatments either for themselves or for their bridal party as part of their wedding package, but this will be at an additional cost. Some packages may offer a bridal spa day or beauty treatments as part of a premium package or as a special promotion.

Here's an overview of the typical hair and makeup service options you might encounter and how to make the most of them.

### Included Services

Some all-inclusive wedding packages may include basic hair and makeup services for the bride as part of the package. These are often limited to a single session on the wedding day, with a predefined style or set of options from which to choose. If included, it's important to discuss the details and limitations of these services early in the planning process to ensure they align with your expectations.

### Upgrade Options

Many all-inclusive resorts offer upgraded beauty services or more extensive packages that can be added to your wedding package for an additional fee. Upgrades might include:

- Trial runs for hair and makeup before the wedding day to finalize your look.
- Advanced styling options, including airbrush makeup or specialized hair techniques.
- Services for the bridal party, including bridesmaids, the mother of the bride, and others.
- Groom and groomsmen grooming services.

## On-Site Salons and Spas

Most all-inclusive resorts with a focus on weddings have on-site salons and spas equipped to handle wedding day beauty needs. Utilizing the on-site salon can offer the convenience of not having to leave the resort and the reassurance of working with professionals familiar with the venue and local climate conditions. Inquire about the salon's portfolio to see examples of their work and ensure their style matches your vision.

## External Vendors

If the resort's offerings don't meet your needs, or if you have a specific stylist in mind, you may consider hiring an external vendor. Some all-inclusive packages allow for external vendors but might require a vendor fee or adherence to certain guidelines. Always check with your wedding coordinator about the resort's policy on external vendors to avoid any misunderstandings.

## Communication and Coordination

Effective communication with your wedding coordinator or the salon manager is crucial to ensure your hair and makeup services go smoothly. Share inspiration pictures, discuss the schedule to ensure there's enough time allocated for all services, and communicate any skin sensitivities or preferences you have. If possible, schedule a consultation or trial session to meet the stylists and discuss your look in detail.

### Planning and Budgeting

When selecting your hair and makeup options, consider how they fit into your overall wedding budget. Upgraded beauty services can vary in cost, so it's essential to get detailed pricing information upfront. Discuss all beauty service options and costs with your wedding coordinator to make informed decisions that align with both your vision and budget.

## 9.4    Groom's Attire and Style

While the spotlight on bridal fashion often overshadows the importance of the groom's attire, selecting the right outfit for the groom is equally crucial in setting the tone for the event and ensuring comfort and style. The groom's attire should reflect the wedding's location, climate, and theme while also complementing the bride's look.

### Considering the Destination's Climate:

The climate of your wedding location plays a pivotal role in choosing suitable attire. For warm, tropical settings, lightweight fabrics such as linen or lightweight wool can keep the groom cool and comfortable. Opting for light colors not only matches the airy vibe of beach or outdoor settings but also helps in staying cool. In contrast, cooler destinations might call for heavier fabrics and layers. A well-tailored wool suit or even tweed can add warmth without sacrificing style, and incorporating accessories like a stylish scarf can elevate the look while providing extra warmth.

**Adapting to the Formality and Style of the Venue:**

The venue's setting dictates the formality of the groom's attire. A beach wedding calls for a more relaxed look, possibly foregoing traditional suits for a smart casual ensemble with tailored trousers and a linen shirt. For ceremonies in grand venues or historic sites, a more formal approach with a classic suit or even a tuxedo can reflect the venue's elegance. The key is to balance comfort with the formality level that the venue inspires.

**Personal Style and Comfort:**

While it's essential to consider the wedding theme and location, the groom's personal style should not be overlooked. The wedding attire should be a reflection of the groom's personality and make him feel confident and comfortable. This could mean adding personal touches through accessories like cufflinks, a pocket square, or a boutonniere that ties in with the wedding's color scheme or theme. Comfort is paramount, especially for destination weddings where the groom may be navigating unfamiliar terrain or weather. Ensuring the attire fits well and is suitable for the day's activities will contribute significantly to the groom's overall experience.

**Coordinating with the Wedding Party:**

The groom's attire should harmonize with the overall wedding party's look. This coordination can be achieved through color schemes, accessories, or specific style elements that tie the groom's look with the groomsmen and the broader wedding theme. Providing clear guidelines on the expected attire for groomsmen and ensuring these complement the groom's outfit will create a cohesive and visually appealing wedding party.

**Planning and Preparation:**

For destination weddings, it's advisable to arrange attire well in advance, considering any local tailoring needs or adjustments. Packing the attire carefully to minimize wrinkles or damage during travel is crucial, and researching local resources for last-minute steaming or adjustments can save stress upon arrival.

# 9.5 Pre-Wedding Beauty Regimen

A comprehensive pre-wedding beauty regimen is a cornerstone of preparing for your big day, especially when the event is set in a location that might present unique challenges for your skin and hair. Initiating this process well ahead of time not only allows for the identification and treatment of any skin or hair concerns but also ensures that you are radiantly ready for your walk down the aisle, regardless of the destination's climate.

## Skin Care

Embarking on a journey to perfect skin begins with a consultation with a dermatologist or esthetician. Such a professional can offer an assessment of your skin's needs and tailor a skincare regimen that addresses any issues such as dryness, oiliness, or acne. Adapting your skincare to the climate of your wedding location is essential; for drier climates, focus on hydration, while oil-free products are best for humid conditions. A high SPF sunscreen is indispensable for sunny locales. Regular, gentle exfoliation, coupled with deep hydration treatments, will enhance your skin's elasticity and radiance, paving the way for a flawless wedding day complexion.

**Hair Care**

A visit to your hairstylist for an assessment can kickstart your hair care regimen. They may suggest treatments to improve hair health, such as deep conditioning or scalp care, ensuring your hair is at its best. If you're contemplating a change in color or style, make these changes months in advance to allow time for any necessary adjustments, ensuring your hair complements your wedding day look perfectly.

**Diet and Exercise**

The role of diet and exercise in your beauty regimen cannot be overstated. A diet rich in antioxidants, omega-3 fatty acids, and essential vitamins can significantly enhance your skin's glow and contribute to your overall health. Complement this with a consistent exercise routine that suits your lifestyle to boost circulation and manage stress, both of which are crucial for achieving that bridal glow.

**Relaxation and Mental Well-being**

Managing stress through yoga, meditation, or regular massages is vital, as stress can adversely affect your skin, hair, and overall health. Equally important is ensuring adequate rest; sleep is crucial for the body's repair processes, and insufficient rest can lead to a lackluster complexion and under-eye circles.

## 9.6    Packing and Transportation Tips

Preparing for a destination wedding involves meticulous packing and transportation planning to ensure all your essentials, especially the delicate items like wedding attire and accessories, arrive safely. Navigating the logistics with a strategy can significantly reduce pre-wedding stress, allowing you to focus on the joy of your upcoming nuptials.

## Wedding Attire

Investing in quality garment bags is crucial for protecting your wedding dress, suit, and any attire for the bridal party. These bags should offer robust protection against moisture and wrinkles. When flying, it's essential to carry your wedding attire on board with you. Airlines often have accommodations for wedding attire, but verifying their policy beforehand is advisable. For items that won't wrinkle as easily, consider rolling them instead of folding and use tissue paper or dry cleaner bags to avoid creases.

## Beauty and Grooming Kits

Transitioning to travel-sized containers for your beauty and grooming essentials not only saves space but also meets airline regulations for liquids in carry-on luggage. Packing a separate toiletry bag for your wedding day necessities ensures you have everything organized, and double-bagging liquids is a good precaution against leaks.

## Accessories and Special Items

Special care should be taken with jewelry and delicate accessories by using a dedicated organizer or small boxes cushioned with bubble wrap, which should be kept with you during travel. Additionally, assembling a wedding day emergency kit with items like safety pins and stain remover can be a lifesaver and should be easily accessible.

## Documentation and Essentials

Keeping essential documents such as passports, travel insurance, and wedding-related paperwork in a secure and reachable place is vital. Creating digital backups and leaving physical copies with someone you trust can provide an extra layer of security.

## Packing Tips for Guests

Offering guests a packing list tailored to the wedding events and destination's climate helps ensure they bring everything they need. Advising the use of durable luggage tags and unique identifiers can help in easily locating their baggage and reducing the chances of loss.

## Transportation Logistics

For transporting bulk items like welcome bags or decorations, shipping to your venue in advance may be the best option. It's important to understand the customs regulations of your destination and choose reliable shipping services. Sometimes, purchasing certain items locally is more practical and cost-effective than transporting them from home, so consider this option to simplify logistics.

# Chapter 10
# Accommodations and
# Logistics

## 10.1  Securing Guest Accommodations

Arranging comfortable and convenient accommodations is a fundamental part of organizing a destination wedding. The right lodging choices can significantly elevate the overall guest experience, turning the event into a memorable getaway for everyone involved.

### Research and Selection

It is recommended to provide a spectrum of lodging options to accommodate the varied budgets and preferences of your guests. This range should span from luxury to budget-friendly choices, ensuring there's a comfortable option for everyone. Ideally, these accommodations should be situated close to your wedding venue to simplify travel arrangements. If the venue is somewhat isolated, consider options within a manageable distance and think about arranging transportation.

### Negotiating Room Blocks

Engaging with hotels near your venue to secure room blocks can be a smart move. This involves reserving a set number of rooms at a discounted rate for your guests. It's crucial to fully understand the terms of this arrangement, including booking deadlines and any penalties for unbooked rooms. Prioritize accommodations that offer flexibility with changes and cancellations, accommodating the evolving plans of your guests.

**Effective Communication**

Ensure your guests have all necessary information regarding accommodation options. Details should include room rates, how to book, contact details, and any booking deadlines, alongside amenities and services provided by the accommodation, such as internet access or breakfast options. Employing your wedding website for disseminating this information, along with a FAQ section, can streamline communication and keep everyone informed.

**Enhancing the Guest Experience**

Welcome bags awaiting guests upon arrival can add a thoughtful touch, packed with essentials and local treats. Such gestures, along with organizing group activities for those staying at the same location, can foster a communal atmosphere, enriching the overall experience.

**Planning for Transportation**

For venues distant from the chosen accommodations, consider arranging shuttle services for the convenience of your guests. This ensures everyone can participate fully in your celebration without the hassle of navigating or parking.

**Addressing Special Needs**

Accommodations should be selected with consideration for any guests with special needs, ensuring facilities are accessible and can cater to specific requirements, such as dietary restrictions. Communicating these needs well in advance allows the accommodations to adequately prepare, ensuring a comfortable stay for all your guests.

## 10.2  Welcome Bags and Local Guides

Welcoming your guests with carefully curated welcome bags and comprehensive local guides is a generous way to enhance their experience at your destination wedding. These thoughtful gestures not only express your appreciation for their attendance but also provide them with essential items and helpful information to enjoy their stay to the fullest.

### Crafting Welcome Bags

Begin with selecting durable and stylish tote bags that can be personalized with your wedding logo, date, or a design that reflects the wedding's locale, making them memorable keepsakes. Fill these bags with local snacks or delicacies, introducing your guests to the flavors of the region. For hydration and refreshment, include bottled water—customized with your wedding details if possible—and perhaps a local wine or craft beer for an adult beverage option. Depending on the destination's climate, consider adding sun protection items like sunscreen and lip balm for sunny locations, or a compact umbrella or cozy scarf for cooler areas. Lastly, a customized map and itinerary provide valuable information for navigating the destination and participating in wedding events.

### Creating Informative Local Guides

An informative local guide should offer recommendations on local attractions, dining, and shopping, enriched with personal anecdotes or tips to make these suggestions more engaging. Include advice on local customs and etiquette, useful phrases for non-English-speaking destinations, and essential emergency contact information, including local services and embassy contacts. Advice on transportation options, with insights into local public transport, reputable taxi services, or rental car recommendations, will greatly assist your guests. Ensure details on transportation arranged for wedding events are also included.

**Packaging and Distribution**

The presentation of the welcome bags should be thoughtful, with consideration for how guests will transport them. A personalized note within each bag can warmly express your gratitude and excitement for their participation in your special day. Strategize the distribution of these welcome bags by coordinating with your accommodations to have them delivered directly to guests' rooms or distributed at check-in. For an added personal touch, greeting guests upon arrival and personally handing out the bags can make for a warm and memorable welcome.

## 10.3 Managing Day-of Logistics

Ensuring the seamless execution of a destination wedding significantly depends on the effective management of day-of logistics. The key to a memorable and stress-free celebration lies in meticulous planning, clear communication, and the ability to adapt.

**Establishing a Clear Timeline**

Creating a detailed itinerary is essential. This schedule should cover all activities, from pre-ceremony preparations through to the ceremony, photo sessions, reception, and any events that follow. Sharing this itinerary with your vendors, wedding party, and guests ensures that everyone is aware of the timing and locations for the day's events.

### Coordinating Transportation

For guest transfers from their accommodations to the venue, confirm and communicate the transportation schedule, including pickup times and locations, while allowing for unexpected delays. Additionally, manage the arrival and setup times for vendors, designating a specific area for their check-in to streamline their setup.

### On-Site Coordination

Appoint a day-of coordinator or a reliable person to manage logistics, acting as a liaison between you, the vendors, and the guests. This individual can address any arising questions or issues. Moreover, an emergency kit containing safety pins, sewing materials, stain removers, and basic first aid supplies can swiftly handle minor mishaps.

### Communication Tools

In venues where cell service may be spotty, walkie-talkies can facilitate communication with your coordination team. Alternatively, a group chat for immediate communication with key wedding party members and vendors can be very effective.

### Handling Unexpected Issues

Adopt a flexible attitude towards unforeseen problems, focusing on solutions. Have contingency plans for critical aspects of the day, such as alternate indoor venues for outdoor activities in case of poor weather, or extra entertainment options to fill any unexpected delays.

### Guest Comfort and Accessibility

Make sure the venue accommodates all guests comfortably, including those with mobility challenges, and consider having staff on hand to assist as necessary.

Depending on the weather and location, comfort stations with fans, heaters, sunscreen, or bug repellent can keep guests comfortable throughout the event.

**Post-Event Logistics**

Arrange for transportation back to accommodations for guests if you've provided transport to the venue. Also, confirm with your vendors the procedures for cleanup and breakdown, ensuring a smooth conclusion to the festivities.

# 10.4  Post-Wedding Logistics

After the celebration of your destination wedding, managing post-wedding logistics is crucial for a smooth transition into married life. This phase involves coordinating with guests, vendors, and handling various tasks that conclude your wedding event effectively. Here's how to ensure that all post-wedding details are addressed efficiently.

**Thanking Your Guests**

A post-wedding gathering, like a brunch, is a wonderful opportunity to personally thank your guests and bid them farewell. It's a gracious closure to the festivities and a gesture of appreciation for their attendance. Following up with personalized thank-you notes for their gifts and shared moments adds a personal and thoughtful touch.

**Managing Vendor Relations and Payments**

Completing all final payments to vendors promptly is essential. Keeping a checklist ensures that no payment is missed. Offering feedback or reviews for your vendors aids in their improvement and guides future couples. Positive experiences can be shared on wedding forums or review platforms to commend their services.

### Handling Rentals and Decor

Organizing the return of rented items, including decor and equipment, is vital to avoid additional charges. Planning for the preservation or disposal of wedding items, such as your bouquet or gown, should be considered well in advance to ensure they are cherished or responsibly managed.

### Legal and Administrative Tasks

Securing your marriage certificate and ensuring it's correctly filed, especially for weddings abroad, is crucial for legal recognition. If a name change is anticipated, begin the process early to update all necessary documents and identifications to reflect your new status.

### Photographs and Wedding Media

Coordinate with your photographer and videographer regarding the delivery timeline for your wedding media. Establish a method for sharing these precious memories with your guests, which could include online albums or social media platforms, allowing everyone to relive the day.

### Reflecting and Reviewing

Taking time to reflect on your wedding with your spouse is valuable for personal memories and future advice for others. Discussing the highlights and areas for improvement enriches your experience. Finally, reviewing your wedding budget against actual expenditures offers insights for your upcoming financial planning as a couple. This reflective process is a meaningful step towards starting your married life on a positive note.

# Chapter 11
# Activities and Excursions

A destination wedding offers a unique opportunity to extend the celebration beyond the ceremony and reception, turning the event into a memorable getaway for you and your guests. Planning group activities and excursions can enhance the experience, allowing everyone to delve deeper into the destination's culture, landscape, and offerings. This chapter will guide you through organizing engaging, enjoyable activities that complement your wedding festivies, ensuring your guests leave with unforgettable memories.

## 11.1  Understanding Your Guests

Planning activities and excursions for a destination wedding necessitates a comprehensive understanding of your guests' interests, abilities, and expectations. This approach not only maximizes their enjoyment and comfort but also cultivates a welcoming atmosphere of inclusivity and appreciation. Here are strategies for effectively discerning your guests' preferences to create an event that's enjoyable for all attendees.

### Surveying Interests and Preferences

Employing pre-wedding surveys can be a valuable tool to collect information regarding your guests' interests, activity preferences, and any specific needs, such as dietary restrictions or mobility considerations. This insight guides your planning, ensuring activities align with guest preferences. Additionally, leveraging your wedding website or social media platforms to discuss potential activities allows for real-time feedback and encourages guests to share their own suggestions, fostering a community spirit among attendees.

### Considerations for Diverse Guest Groups

Recognizing the varying age ranges and physical capabilities within your guest list is essential. Activities should cater to all guests, from child-friendly options to pursuits that appeal to the more adventurous. It's important to ensure activities are accessible to everyone, incorporating both low-impact and more physically demanding choices. Being mindful of the cultural backgrounds and sensitivities of your guests is also crucial, as activities should be respectful and inclusive to all.

### Budget Considerations

Transparency about the costs associated with each activity, particularly if guests are expected to contribute, is key. Offering activities at various price points allows guests to participate according to their budget. Whenever possible, negotiate group discounts for activities to make them more affordable and encourage wider participation.

### Flexibility and Options

Providing a broad selection of activities—from leisurely social events and cultural excursions to adventurous outings—ensures that there's something for everyone. It's equally important to allow enough free time in the schedule for guests to unwind or explore on their own. Avoid over-scheduling, as guests often appreciate the opportunity to experience the destination at their leisure, ensuring a memorable and personalized experience for each attendee.

## 11.2 Planning Diverse Activities

Enhancing your destination wedding with a range of activities that appeal to the different interests of your guests can significantly elevate their experience. Whether it's through leisurely explorations, cultural deep-dives, or exciting adventures, the aim is to present a well-rounded selection that encourages participation and fosters memorable moments.

### Welcome and Social Gatherings

Initiate the wedding celebrations with a welcoming mixer, setting the tone for the festivities. This event can range from a simple cocktail hour to a more elaborate welcome dinner that showcases local cuisine, offering guests a chance to socialize in a laid-back environment. Further, hosting group dinners or themed nights centered around the local culinary and cultural landscape provides a cozy space for guests to bond and indulge in the destination's offerings together.

### Cultural and Local Experiences

Organizing guided tours to explore notable landmarks or cultural institutions adds an enriching layer to the wedding experience, combining education with entertainment. Offering workshops or classes, such as cooking or dancing, led by local experts allows guests to immerse themselves in the destination's culture, providing hands-on experiences that are both unique and memorable.

### Adventure and Outdoor Activities

For the thrill-seekers in your group, planning outdoor excursions that leverage the natural beauty of your destination can satisfy their adventurous urges. Activities like hiking, snorkeling, or zip-lining cater to those with a penchant for exploration. Incorporating group sports or recreational activities adds a fun competitive twist to the celebrations, fostering camaraderie among guests.

### Relaxation and Leisure

A group spa day offers a serene escape for guests, allowing them to rejuvenate amidst the wedding festivities. Alternatively, dedicating a day for relaxation at the beach or poolside, equipped with games and refreshments, creates a leisurely space for guests to chill and recharge.

### Considerations for Planning

When scheduling activities, it's crucial to consider the overall wedding timeline, ensuring activities are well-spaced and communicated clearly to guests. Arranging transportation for off-site activities and ensuring venues are accessible to everyone are key logistical aspects. Communicate activity details effectively, perhaps through your wedding website or a dedicated communication channel, allowing guests to plan accordingly. Offering activities as optional encourages guests to tailor their experience to their liking, ensuring that everyone has the most enjoyable time possible.

## 11.3 Effective Scheduling and Logistics

The success of a destination wedding's accompanying activities hinges on well-thought-out scheduling and meticulous logistical planning. Striking a perfect balance between organized events and sufficient relaxation time ensures that guests can fully enjoy each moment without feeling overwhelmed.

**Developing a Thoughtful Itinerary**

Creating a balanced itinerary is crucial. It should weave together structured events with plenty of opportunities for guests to explore independently or unwind. This careful planning prevents the itinerary from becoming congested and ensures that guests have a fulfilling yet relaxing experience. When planning the timing of activities, consider the local climate and any cultural events that might influence your plans, scheduling activities to maximize comfort and participation.

**Managing Transportation**

Organizing group transportation for events situated away from the main accommodations or venue is essential. This approach eases travel concerns for guests, particularly those unfamiliar with the destination. It's important to clearly outline transportation schedules, including all relevant pickup and drop-off details, making this information accessible through various channels such as your wedding website or detailed itineraries.

**Facilitating Guest Coordination**

Setting up a centralized information resource, either through a digital platform or a physical location, helps guests stay informed about the schedule and any logistical details or updates. Providing on-site assistance through a dedicated coordinator can be invaluable, offering direct support to guests and addressing any sudden changes or needs that may arise.

**Subsidizing and Group Discounts**

If your budget allows, consider subsidizing part of the cost for more expensive activities to make them more accessible to your guests. Even a partial subsidy can be a significant gesture that enables more guests to join.

Leverage the size of your group to negotiate discounts for activities and excursions. Group rates can make activities more affordable, and sharing these savings with your guests can encourage broader participation.

**Handling Payments and Reservations**

Transparent communication regarding any costs associated with the activities, and whether they are included in the wedding package or require an additional fee, helps guests manage their budgets effectively. Ensure that reservations for group activities are made in advance and reconfirmed closer to the date, securing all logistical arrangements and informing guests of what to expect.

**Incorporating Feedback and Making Adjustments**

Being receptive to guest feedback during the wedding events can provide valuable insights for on-the-fly adjustments to the schedule or logistics, enhancing the overall experience. Additionally, having contingency plans for activities that may be impacted by unpredictable elements, such as weather, and communicating any necessary changes promptly ensures that the celebration remains enjoyable for everyone involved.

# Chapter 12
# The Honeymoon

After the excitement and hustle of planning and celebrating your destination wedding, the honeymoon is your time to unwind, reflect, and bask in the bliss of your new marital status. Whether you choose to extend your stay at the wedding destination or jet off to another locale, this chapter of your journey together should be about connection, relaxation, and creating unforgettable memories.

## 12.1 Seamless Transition from Wedding to Honeymoon

Effortlessly transitioning from the celebratory atmosphere of your wedding to the tranquil intimacy of your honeymoon is key to starting your married life on the right note. This requires strategic planning to ensure you and your partner can smoothly shift gears from the high energy of your special day to the relaxed, romantic vibe of your honeymoon.

### Planning for Post-Wedding

Allow yourselves a grace period after the wedding festivities to unwind and mentally prepare for the honeymoon. Taking a day or even a few hours to relax post-wedding can help you both reflect on the joyous event and ready yourselves for the honeymoon adventure ahead. Organizing your luggage in advance, with separate sets for the wedding and the honeymoon, especially if different attire or gear is required, can streamline the transition and minimize post-celebration stress.

### Staying at the Wedding Destination

If you choose to remain at your wedding location for the honeymoon, a change in scenery within the same destination can symbolize the start of this new chapter. Transitioning to a different hotel or a more secluded setting can provide a fresh backdrop for your honeymoon. Planning unique activities distinct from those of the wedding, such as romantic outings or indulgent spa sessions, further delineates this new phase from the wedding celebrations.

### Transitioning to a New Destination

For those venturing to a new destination, managing travel details well in advance is crucial. Ensuring a smooth journey involves pre-arranging all travel logistics, from airport transfers to accommodations. On your first day, adopt a relaxed pace with minimal plans to allow yourselves to absorb the new surroundings and begin your honeymoon on a restful note.

### Communicating with Guests

A gesture of farewell or personalized thank-you notes to your wedding guests acknowledges their part in your celebration and signals your transition to the honeymoon. This can be a thoughtful way to conclude the wedding festivities and set the stage for your departure.

### Managing Expectations

Establishing clear boundaries with friends and family regarding your availability during the honeymoon is important for preserving this special time. While it's beneficial to have a planned itinerary, remaining adaptable allows you to cherish unexpected moments and the simple pleasure of each other's company, ensuring a memorable start to your life together.

## 12.2 Extending Your Stay: Honeymooning at Your Wedding Destination

Choosing to extend your stay for your honeymoon at the wedding destination can enrich your experience, making the transition from wedding guests to honeymooners both smooth and memorable. This decision simplifies travel arrangements, potentially reduces expenses, and provides a deeper immersion into the locale's ambiance and offerings. Here are strategies to maximize the benefits of staying at your wedding destination for your honeymoon.

### Advantages of Staying Put

Opting to remain in the same destination for your honeymoon simplifies planning, removing the hassle of additional travel arrangements and allowing you to ease into honeymoon bliss right after your wedding festivities. Your familiarity with the locale, gained during the wedding preparations and celebration, equips you with knowledge about the best places to visit, dine, and relax, enabling a more enriching and confident exploration of the area during your honeymoon.

### Transitioning from Wedding to Honeymoon

A change in your accommodation post-wedding can signify the beginning of your honeymoon phase, offering a fresh backdrop for this new chapter. Seeking out special experiences that differ from your wedding activities—like a secluded dinner under the stars, a private tour of a hidden gem, or a couple's spa day—can help distinguish your honeymoon from the wedding, making it uniquely memorable.

### Practical Considerations

When arranging your wedding stay, explore potential honeymoon packages or extended stay discounts with your accommodations to optimize your budget. Communicating the end of wedding festivities and the start of your honeymoon to guests is crucial for setting boundaries, ensuring you have the privacy and space needed to celebrate your new marriage. Packing for a range of activities is also important, ensuring you're prepared for both relaxation and adventure without the need to repack or sort through wedding attire.

### Making It Special

Consider a post-wedding photoshoot to capture your honeymoon moments in a setting that's become significant to you both, adding a relaxed and personalized touch to your wedding album. Delve into local experiences you may have overlooked during the wedding rush—unique dining spots, cultural sites, or natural wonders—to add depth and discovery to your honeymoon. Above all, allocate time to unwind, reminisce about your wedding highlights, and savor the start of your married life together, taking full advantage of the extended stay to appreciate each moment fully.

## 12.3  Nearby Honeymoon Destinations: A Blend of Adventure and Convenience

Opting for a honeymoon destination close to your wedding venue can enrich your post-wedding experience with minimal travel fuss, offering the perfect combination of discovery and ease. Such choices allow you to immerse yourselves in a new environment while avoiding the complexities of long-distance travel. Here's how to select a nearby honeymoon spot that promises a delightful commencement to your matrimonial journey.

## Exploring Regional Gems

Investigate the hidden treasures within easy reach of your wedding site. Whether it's an undiscovered beach, a charming mountain village, or a tranquil spot in the countryside, choosing a location with a different vibe from your wedding can instantly set the tone for a distinct honeymoon phase. Additionally, destinations rich in cultural offerings provide an opportunity to dive into local arts, history, and traditions, enriching your honeymoon with meaningful experiences.

## Embracing Nature and Adventure

Destinations endowed with natural beauty—be it national parks, reserves, or picturesque coastlines—serve as ideal backdrops for couples keen on outdoor adventures. These locales offer countless activities, from hiking and snorkeling to kayaking, fostering memorable experiences in the embrace of nature. Alternatively, wellness retreats or spa resorts can provide a serene setting for relaxation and reflection, marking a peaceful start to your life together.

## Considerations for Selecting a Nearby Destination

When choosing your honeymoon spot, consider travel time to ensure it's easily accessible, thereby reducing transit stress and environmental impact. A destination offering a climatic or seasonal change can significantly differentiate your honeymoon from your wedding, adding a layer of novelty. Moreover, a place known for its distinctive culinary scene or local crafts can offer unique experiences, deepening your connection to the locale.

**Seamless Transition Tips**

Planning your honeymoon transition alongside your wedding logistics can facilitate a smooth changeover. Advanced booking of accommodations and activities eliminates last-minute scrambles, ensuring a serene start to your honeymoon. Packing for both the wedding and honeymoon, particularly when the destinations have varied climates or dress codes, requires thoughtful preparation. You might also consider luggage forwarding services to ease the journey between your wedding and honeymoon venues. Introducing a surprise element, either through keeping the destination a secret or planning a surprise activity upon arrival, can add an exciting twist to your post-wedding adventure.

## 12.4  Experiences Over Things: Enriching Your Honeymoon Journey

The commencement of your shared life story with the words "I do" ushers in an era of adventures, the first of which is your honeymoon. This journey is far more than a mere vacation; it's a golden opportunity to weave together a tapestry of memories that will enrich your marriage for years to come. Emphasizing experiences over material possessions during your honeymoon can deepen your bond and provide you with cherished stories. Here's how to ensure your honeymoon is not only unforgettable but also transformative.

**Crafting Unforgettable Moments**

Engaging in activities that challenge and excite you both, like scuba diving, hot air ballooning, or exploring a foreign cuisine through a cooking class, can significantly strengthen your relationship and leave you with enduring memories. Immersing yourselves in the local culture by attending traditional performances, participating in festivals, or volunteering allows for a deeper connection with each other and the world.

## Personalizing Your Experiences

It's essential to tailor your honeymoon activities to reflect your shared passions, whether that's history, gastronomy, or the great outdoors. Planning a distinctive, destination-specific experience that speaks to your journey as a couple can add a deeply personal touch to your adventure, making it truly one-of-a-kind.

## Savoring Each Moment

Adopting a slow travel mindset, where you immerse yourselves in fewer places but with more depth, can enhance your appreciation of each experience. Documenting your journey, whether through a shared journal, photographs, or collecting souvenirs, ensures you keep a tangible record of these precious moments.

## Learning and Growing Together

Seek out educational opportunities that also entertain, such as attending workshops, tours, or lessons in something new. These experiences not only bond you further but also contribute to your mutual growth. Taking time to reflect on and discuss each experience can deepen your understanding of one another and the journey you're on together.

## Prioritizing Experiences in Planning

When budgeting for your honeymoon, prioritize allocating resources towards experiences rather than things. This focus ensures your funds contribute to building lasting memories. Additionally, soliciting recommendations from locals or acquaintances can guide you to the most impactful and authentic activities, enhancing the richness of your honeymoon experience.

## 12.5 Embracing Relaxation and Rejuvenation on Your Honeymoon

If you want to turn your honeymoon into a sanctuary of tranquility and a time for deep rejuvenation, consider it a peaceful interlude that offers the opportunity to relax, rejuvenate, and joyfully mark the beginning of your married life. Emphasizing relaxation and renewal is crucial for replenishing your well-being and strengthening the connection between you as newlyweds..

**Wellness as a Priority**

Booking a segment of your honeymoon at a spa or wellness retreat can be incredibly beneficial. These havens provide couples' treatments such as massages, facials, and holistic therapies designed to foster relaxation and health. Integrating mindful practices into your honeymoon, like morning yoga, meditation, or quiet time in nature, can also play a significant role in centering and connecting you as a couple.

**Crafting a Serene Environment**

Selecting tranquil accommodations is crucial for unwinding. Opt for a secluded spot—be it a beach villa, a woodland cabin, or a luxury suite with a private view—that guarantees peace. A digital detox, by consciously choosing to limit technology use, further ensures that you immerse yourselves in each other's company and the tranquil ambiance around you.

### Indulging in Simple Pleasures

Take pleasure in leisurely dining experiences, whether it's a candlelit dinner, a picnic with a view, or a tasting menu exploring local cuisines, to truly appreciate the joy of eating together. Immersing yourselves in nature—be it beach walks, forest hikes, or gentle boat rides—serves as a rejuvenating backdrop to your connection, inviting tranquility into your relationship.

### Incorporating Ample Downtime

Ensuring your itinerary includes plenty of downtime for rest—like lazy mornings, afternoon naps, or evenings under the stars—makes relaxation an integral part of your honeymoon. Leave space for impromptu leisure, as the most restful moments often stem from unplanned, quiet togetherness in a beautiful locale.

### Fostering Emotional Intimacy

The secluded setting of your honeymoon is ideal for engaging in meaningful conversations about your aspirations, hopes, and plans, thus deepening your emotional intimacy. Taking time to express gratitude for each other and reflect on your shared journey and achievements can also be a source of rejuvenation.

### Choosing Rejuvenating Activities

When planning your activities, opt for those that rejuvenate rather than exhaust. Activities like gentle cycling, visiting therapeutic hot springs, or engaging in cultural exploration can enrich your honeymoon experience without leading to fatigue, ensuring that your time together is as restorative as it is memorable.

## 12.6　Making It Special

Your honeymoon is more than the inaugural trip you embark on as a married couple; it's an intimately personal celebration of your union, ripe with opportunities to forge enduring memories. Elevating your honeymoon beyond a simple getaway to a memorable voyage of love and discovery involves incorporating personalized elements, surprises, and deeply connecting experiences. Here's how to transform your honeymoon into an extraordinary adventure.

**Tailoring Your Journey**

Creating a customized itinerary that mirrors your shared interests, aspirations, and passions is key. Whether it's arranging for a private viewing at an art gallery for art aficionados, a gourmet cooking class for culinary enthusiasts, or an isolated nature hike for outdoor lovers, these activities should echo your journey as a couple. Introducing themed days can also add depth, with each day reflecting a significant aspect of your relationship, such as reenacting your first date or visiting settings from beloved films.

**Surprises and Gestures of Love**

Incorporating surprise elements or activities adds a layer of excitement and anticipation. Imagine organizing a secret sunset cruise or a dinner at a stunning location unknown to your partner. Moreover, small but heartfelt gestures, like leaving love notes in surprise locations, can profoundly enhance the romantic ambiance of your honeymoon.

**Commemorative Keepsakes**

Opt for souvenirs that hold personal meaning over generic ones. This might include local art, a piece of jewelry featuring a gemstone from the region, or a specially crafted memento of your trip. Consider booking a professional photo session to capture the beauty of your destination and your moments as a couple, offering timeless memories of your love in a breathtaking backdrop.

### Crafting Shared Memories

Maintaining a honeymoon journal allows both partners to document their daily experiences, thoughts, and emotions, creating a treasured record of the journey. Emphasizing the collection of moments over material things encourages mindfulness and appreciation for each shared experience, from serene mornings to exhilarating new ventures.

### Embracing Luxury and Leisure

Allow yourselves moments of splendor and pampering with luxurious indulgences, such as staying in a sumptuous suite, dining at a renowned restaurant, or enjoying a lavish spa day. These indulgences make your honeymoon even more memorable.

### Prioritizing Quality Time

Ultimately, the significance of your honeymoon lies in the uninterrupted, focused time spent together. It's about connecting, reflecting on your shared past, and dreaming about your future, making every moment count towards strengthening your bond as you embark on life's journey together.

## 12.7  Health and Safety

Ensuring health and safety during your honeymoon is crucial, especially when venturing into new and unfamiliar territories. Proper planning and taking the right precautions can safeguard you against potential health risks, making your trip both enjoyable and stress-free. Here's how to keep health and safety at the forefront without diminishing the romance and adventure of your honeymoon.

## Preparing for Health Before Travel

Before setting off, it's wise to consult with a travel medicine specialist or your regular healthcare provider. They can offer invaluable advice on vaccinations, medications, and health precautions tailored to your destination. Securing comprehensive travel insurance that covers medical treatment, evacuation, and trip cancellations due to health reasons is also essential. Preparing a health kit with prescription medications, over-the-counter remedies, hand sanitizer, insect repellent, sunscreen, and any other items recommended by your healthcare provider is a must.

## Food and Water Precautions

Understanding the food and water safety standards of your honeymoon destination is crucial. In some locales, it's best to steer clear of tap water, ice from tap water, and certain raw foods to avoid illness. When eating out, opt for food that's freshly prepared in reputable establishments and exercise caution with street food or buffet items that might have been exposed to the elements for too long.

## Environmental Consciousness

Protecting yourselves from the sun by using broad-spectrum sunscreen, wearing protective clothing, and seeking shade during the sun's peak hours is vital to prevent sunburn and heat-related issues. If traveling to areas with mosquito-borne diseases, applying insect repellent, using mosquito nets, and wearing protective clothing during dusk and dawn are key preventative measures.

**Ensuring Personal Safety and Security**

Staying updated on local news and any travel advisories for your destination is crucial for personal safety. In places where it's advised, registering with your embassy or consulate can add an extra layer of security. It's also important to use hotel safes for valuables and documents and remain vigilant about your belongings and surroundings, especially in crowded or unfamiliar areas.

**Emergency Readiness**

Having a list of local emergency contacts, including hospitals, ambulance services, and your country's embassy or consulate, is indispensable. Creating an emergency communication plan with your partner, ensuring your phones are charged and equipped with emergency numbers, and utilizing location-sharing apps can enhance your safety.

# Chapter 13
# Real Destination Wedding Stories

## 13.1 Real Stories

Celebrating love through a destination wedding offers couples a unique and memorable way to begin their married life together. Each destination wedding carries its own set of adventures, challenges, and unforgettable moments. In this chapter, we delve into real destination wedding stories from couples who ventured near and far to say "I do." Their experiences shed light on the magic, mishaps, and meaningful lessons learned, providing inspiration and insights for couples planning their own destination nuptials.

**Jenna and Alex's Rocky Mountain Adventure**

Jenna and Alex decided to eschew a traditional wedding for an intimate elopement in the Rocky Mountains. Accompanied only by their closest family members, a photographer, and an officiant, they exchanged vows at sunrise, overlooking a breathtaking mountain vista. The serenity and beauty of the moment were unmatched, though the day was not without its challenges, including a minor hiking injury and unexpected wildlife encounters. Their story highlights the beauty of simplicity and the importance of embracing the unexpected.

**Maria and David's Caribbean Dream**

Choosing a picturesque beach in the Caribbean, Maria and David's wedding was the epitome of tropical paradise, complete with steel drum music and a sea breeze. However, a sudden rainstorm forced the ceremony to move indoors. Despite this, the couple and their guests danced the night away, proving that a change in plans could lead to new, joyous experiences. Their story is a testament to the power of positivity and the magic of rain on a wedding day - considered good luck by many cultures.

### Anika and Rohan's Blend of Traditions

Anika and Rohan celebrated their union in Italy, merging their Indian and Italian heritages into a vibrant, multicultural ceremony. From a traditional Baraat with a vintage Italian car to a fusion menu that delighted guests, their wedding was a beautiful representation of two families' cultures coming together. Challenges included language barriers with local vendors and coordinating logistics for guests traveling from across the globe. Their story underscores the beauty of cultural fusion and the importance of clear communication in planning.

### Eleanor and Miguel's Step Back in Time

Eleanor and Miguel's love for history led them to a stunning 19th-century mansion in France for their wedding venue. They incorporated historical details into every aspect of their wedding, from the decor to the attire, creating an immersive experience for their guests. A local labor strike posed logistical challenges, but the community's support helped overcome obstacles, adding a layer of memorable solidarity to their celebration. Their wedding illustrates how a shared passion can transform a wedding into an unforgettable experience.

### Hannah and Sam's Rustic Elegance

Set in a lush vineyard, Hannah and Sam's wedding combined rustic charm with elegant details. The rolling hills and rows of grapevines offered a stunning backdrop for their vows and photos. A last-minute caterer cancellation tested their resilience, but a local family-owned restaurant stepped in, providing a meal that became one of the day's highlights. This story emphasizes the importance of community support and the unexpected joys that can arise from unforeseen changes.

### Sophia and Luca's Italian Idyll

Sophia and Luca chose an ancient villa nestled in the heart of Tuscany for their wedding, drawn by Luca's Italian heritage and their shared love of the region's rustic beauty. The villa's vine-covered terraces and panoramic views of rolling hills set the stage for a wedding that was both intimate and breathtaking. A local folk band, discovered during one of their planning visits, provided an authentic soundtrack to the festivities. The challenge came when an unexpected heatwave swept through the area, but quick thinking and local connections allowed them to source elegant parasols and hand fans that not only provided relief but also added a stylish touch to their celebration. Sophia and Luca's wedding was a testament to embracing local culture and the importance of adaptability.

### Fiona and Ewan's Scottish Soirée

Fiona and Ewan, embracing their Scottish roots, invited friends and family to a historic castle in the Scottish Highlands. Their ceremony, held in the castle's ancient chapel, was followed by a lively reception featuring a ceilidh band and traditional Scottish fare. The misty highland weather, which could have dampened spirits, instead added a magical touch to their photographs and the overall ambiance. The couple provided guests with custom tartan blankets, a cozy and thoughtful gesture that was much appreciated. Their story highlights how weather can contribute to the atmosphere of a destination wedding and the value of incorporating traditional elements to celebrate heritage.

**Cara and Jordan's Coastal Charm**

Opting for a laid-back yet elegant vibe, Cara and Jordan chose a seaside resort in the Maldives for their wedding, with a ceremony set against the backdrop of turquoise waters and white sandy beaches. Their day was filled with personalized details, from a sand blending ceremony to signify their union to a boat trip for guests to explore the stunning coral reefs. The biggest challenge arose from a last-minute flight cancellation for their photographer. Resourcefulness led them to a local photographer whose underwater photography skills captured breathtaking moments from their boat excursion. This adventure underscored the beauty of serendipity and the unique memories that come from unexpected changes.

## 13.2   Lessons Learned and Advice Shared

Drawing inspiration from the essence of various destination wedding stories, whether real or imagined, there are invaluable lessons to be learned and pieces of advice that can benefit future couples planning their journey down the aisle in a far-flung locale. Here's a compilation of lessons learned and advice shared, distilled from the experiences of couples who have navigated the beautiful complexities of destination weddings.

**Embrace Flexibility and Adaptability**

- **Lesson**: No matter how meticulously you plan, unexpected changes can and will occur. Weather, vendor availability, and local conditions can all throw unforeseen challenges your way.

- **Advice**: Approach your wedding planning with flexibility. Be ready to adjust your plans and remember that sometimes, plan B turns out even better than plan A. The ability to adapt with grace can transform potential stressors into unique elements that make your wedding unforgettable.

## Prioritize Communication

- **Lesson**: Clear and ongoing communication with your partner, guests, vendors, and on-site coordinators is crucial. Misunderstandings and assumptions can lead to complications and disappointments.

- **Advice**: Establish regular check-ins with all parties involved in your wedding planning. Use tools and technology to streamline communication and ensure everyone is on the same page regarding expectations and logistics.

## Invest in Local Expertise

- **Lesson**: Local vendors and wedding planners bring invaluable insight into the destination's logistics, culture, and best-kept secrets. Their knowledge can be the key to unlocking experiences and solutions you might not have considered.

- **Advice**: Leverage the expertise of locals, from planners to vendors. Their understanding of the area and professional network can help you navigate challenges more efficiently and enrich your wedding with authentic local touches.


## Mind Your Guests' Experience

- **Lesson**: The comfort and experience of your guests are integral to the overall success of your destination wedding. From travel logistics to accommodations and activities, the guest experience requires thoughtful consideration.

- **Advice**: Provide detailed information about the destination, including a list of activities, accommodations, and a clear itinerary. Consider arranging group transportation and accommodations, and perhaps plan a welcome event to make your guests feel valued and included.


## Incorporate Personal Touches

- **Lesson**: The most memorable weddings are those infused with personal touches that reflect the couple's story, interests, and journey together.

- **Advice**: Find ways to personalize your wedding, from the choice of venue to the ceremony and decor. These personal touches not only make your wedding stand out but also create a more intimate and meaningful experience for you and your guests.

**Plan for Downtime**

- **Lesson**: The excitement of a destination wedding can quickly turn into exhaustion without proper pacing. An overly packed schedule can leave little room for the couple and guests to truly relax and savor the experience.

- **Advice**: Incorporate downtime into your wedding itinerary, allowing you and your guests to relax, explore, or simply enjoy some leisure time. This balance is key to ensuring that everyone has an enjoyable and rejuvenating experience.

**Focus on the Big Picture**

- **Lesson**: It's easy to get caught up in the details and stress of wedding planning, especially when it's in a different country or culture.

- **Advice**: Keep the focus on what truly matters: celebrating your love and commitment in the company of those you cherish. When challenges arise, remind yourself of the bigger picture. The imperfections often lead to the most cherished memories.

**Document the Journey**

- **Lesson**: The whirlwind of activities and emotions can make the wedding and honeymoon pass by in a blur.

- **Advice**: Ensure you document your journey, both through professional photography/videography and personal notes or keepsakes. These mementos will be invaluable in reliving and cherishing your destination wedding experience for years to come.

# Appendix:
# Popular Destinations

## ❖ Caribbean Islands (e.g., Jamaica, Bahamas)

**Pros:**
- Stunning beaches and clear blue waters offer a picturesque backdrop.
- Many all-inclusive resorts simplify planning and budgeting.
- Favorable weather most of the year.

**Cons:**
- Hurricane season (June to November) can pose risks.
- Popular spots may be crowded, especially during peak season.

**Who It's For:**
- Couples looking for a tropical beach wedding with a laid-back vibe and those desiring an all-inclusive experience.

## ❖ Tuscany, Italy

**Pros:**
- Breathtaking landscapes, historic sites, and world-renowned cuisine.
- Offers a romantic and culturally rich atmosphere.
- Abundance of vineyards for wine-loving couples.

**Cons:**
- Can be expensive, from venues to accommodations.

- The popularity of the region might mean booking well in advance.

**Who It's For:**
- Food and wine enthusiasts, history buffs, and those seeking a romantic, picturesque setting.


## ❖   Bali, Indonesia

**Pros:**
- Offers a unique blend of beautiful beaches, lush landscapes, and vibrant culture.
- Variety of venue options, from luxurious beach resorts to private villas.
- Relatively affordable compared to other destination wedding locales.

**Cons:**
- Long travel time for guests coming from far away, which might affect attendance.
- Humidity and rainy season could impact outdoor events.

**Who It's For:**
- Adventure-seeking couples and those drawn to exotic locations with a spiritual and cultural richness.


## ❖   Paris, France

**Pros:**
- Known as the "City of Love," providing an inherently romantic setting.
- Iconic landmarks and exquisite cuisine.

- Rich in art, history, and fashion.

**Cons:**
- High cost for accommodations, venues, and services.
- Navigating the city and language barrier can be challenging for guests.

**Who It's For:**
- Couples dreaming of a classic, sophisticated urban wedding with a touch of romance and luxury.

## ❖ Maui, Hawaii

**Pros:**
- Diverse natural beauty, including beaches, volcanoes, and rainforests.
- Welcoming culture with unique traditions to incorporate into your wedding.
- No passport required for U.S. residents.

**Cons:**
- Higher price point due to its popularity and remote location.
- Limited accommodation options during peak tourist seasons.

**Who It's For:**
- Nature lovers and those wishing to incorporate natural beauty and traditional Hawaiian elements into their ceremony.

## ❖ Santorini, Greece

**Pros:**
- Spectacular sunsets and iconic white and blue buildings create a stunning backdrop.
- Delicious Mediterranean cuisine.
- Rich historical sites and vibrant local culture.

**Cons:**
- The island's terrain and stairs can be challenging for guests with mobility issues.
- Peak season crowds and costs.

**Who It's For:**
- Couples looking for a romantic and picturesque setting with historical and cultural depth.

## ❖ Banff, Canada

**Pros:**
- Breathtaking mountain landscapes and pristine lakes.
- Great for outdoor adventures and nature activities.
- Relatively easy accessibility from major Canadian and U.S. cities.

**Cons:**
- Cooler weather, even in summer, might not suit all guests.
- National park regulations may limit venue choices and guest activities.

**Who It's For:**
- Outdoor enthusiasts and those seeking a majestic mountain setting for their nuptials.

## ❖   Amalfi Coast, Italy

**Pros:**
- Stunning coastal cliffs and Mediterranean architecture offer breathtaking views.
- Renowned Italian cuisine and fresh seafood.
- Rich in culture and history, with plenty of exploration opportunities.

**Cons:**
- The rugged terrain may not be suitable for all guests, especially those with mobility issues.
- High demand and relatively high cost for venues and accommodations.

**Who It's For:**
- Couples desiring a romantic, picturesque seaside wedding with gourmet dining experiences.


## ❖   Kyoto, Japan

**Pros:**
- Offers a blend of traditional and modern, with ancient temples and beautiful gardens.
- Unique cultural experiences, from tea ceremonies to geisha performances.
- Cherry blossom season provides a stunning natural backdrop.

**Cons:**
- Language barrier and cultural differences might pose planning challenges.
- Costs can be high, and the city can be crowded, especially during cherry blossom season.

**Who It's For:**
- Couples fascinated by cultural richness and those seeking a blend of tradition and natural beauty in a sophisticated urban setting.


## ❖ Cancun, Mexico

**Pros:**
- Easily reachable from most parts of North America, making it convenient for guests.
- Abundance of options that can simplify planning and budgeting.
- Offers picturesque ceremonies with turquoise waters as the backdrop.

**Cons:**
- May to November can be risky with unpredictable weather during the hurricane season.
- Being a popular tourist destination, it might not feel as exclusive or private.

**Who It's For:**
- Couples looking for a hassle-free, beachfront wedding with all-inclusive convenience and vibrant nightlife.


## ❖ Phuket, Thailand

**Pros:**
- As one of the world's most beautiful beaches, Phuket offers picturesque settings for beach weddings.
- Offers luxurious experiences at a fraction of the cost compared to other destinations.

- Traditional Thai ceremonies and hospitality can make weddings truly unique.

**Cons:**
- Travel can be lengthy and expensive from the Americas and Europe.
- Being a popular tourist destination, some areas of Phuket can be crowded.

**Who It's For:**
- Adventurous couples drawn to exotic landscapes, cultural richness, and those seeking value for luxury.

## ❖ Prague, Czech Republic

**Pros:**
- Historic architecture and cobblestone streets offer a romantic and enchanting backdrop.
- Easy access for guests traveling from within Europe.
- Compared to Western European cities, Prague offers affordable luxury.

**Cons:**
- Popular tourist destination, especially in summer, can affect privacy and photos.
- While widely spoken, English is not universal, potentially complicating arrangements.

**Who It's For:**
- Couples who dream of a historical or fairytale-like wedding in a city that blends medieval charm with modern vibrancy.

## ❖ Cape Town, South Africa

**Pros:**
- Diverse landscapes, including beaches, mountains, and vineyards.
- Rich wildlife and unique adventure activities (e.g., safari tours, shark cage diving).
- Vibrant local culture and cuisine.

**Cons:**
- Long travel distance for guests coming from certain regions.
- Safety concerns in certain areas require careful planning and advisories.

**Who It's For:**
- Adventure-loving couples and nature enthusiasts looking for a dynamic and diverse destination.

## ❖ Reykjavik, Iceland

**Pros:**
- Otherworldly landscapes, including waterfalls, glaciers, and volcanic fields.
- Opportunity for unique experiences like the Northern Lights or hot spring baths.
- Midnight sun offers extended daylight for summer weddings.

**Cons:**
- Weather can be unpredictable and often chilly, even in summer.
- Iceland's popularity has led to increased costs for travel and weddings.

**Who It's For:**

- Couples looking for an adventurous wedding in a unique, dramatic natural setting, embracing the elements as part of their experience.

## ❖ Marrakech, Morocco

**Pros:**

- Rich cultural tapestry, vibrant markets (souks), and stunning Moorish architecture.
- Variety of venue options, from luxury riads to desert oases.
- Exceptional local cuisine and hospitality.

**Cons:**

- Summer temperatures can be extremely hot.
- Navigating local customs and logistics might require expert assistance.

**Who It's For:**

- Couples enchanted by exotic cultures and those desiring a colorful, sensory-rich celebration.

## ❖ Queenstown, New Zealand

**Pros:**

- Offers breathtaking landscapes of lakes, mountains, and rivers.
- Known as the adventure capital, it's perfect for thrill-seeking couples (bungy jumping, skydiving).
- Mild climate year-round and English-speaking country, easing communication.

**Cons:**

- Distance and travel costs may be prohibitive for some guests.
- Popular tourist destination, which can affect availability and prices.

**Who It's For:**

- Outdoorsy couples and adrenaline junkies wanting a scenic backdrop and activities for every guest.

## ❖ Edinburgh, Scotland

**Pros:**

- Rich historical and cultural setting with stunning castles and medieval architecture.
- Scottish traditions can add unique elements to the wedding (bagpipers, kilts).
- Generally cooler climate, appealing for those preferring milder weather.

**Cons:**

- Weather can be unpredictable, with rain a frequent possibility.
- Some historical venues may have restrictions or require early booking due to popularity.

**Who It's For:**

- Couples drawn to historic charm and cultural traditions, seeking a fairy-tale setting with a touch of majesty.

## ❖ Fiji

**Pros:**
- Unparalleled natural beauty and the warmth of its people.
- Offers a variety of wedding venues from intimate beachfront ceremonies to luxurious resort settings.
- Traditional music and dance can add a unique touch to your celebration.

**Cons:**
- Remote location means longer travel times for guests coming from afar, which could affect attendance.
- The tropical climate also brings a risk of rain, particularly during the wet season (November to April).

**Who It's For:**
- Couples dreaming of a tropical paradise wedding, complete with breathtaking sunsets and a laid-back island vibe. It's perfect for those wanting a more intimate, nature-centric ceremony with a touch of local culture.

## ❖ Dubai, United Arab Emirates

**Pros:**
- Offers a blend of modern luxury and traditional Arabian culture.
- From towering skyscrapers and glamorous hotels to serene desert resorts, the city provides a range of unforgettable venues.
- Known for its exceptional service standards, ensuring a seamless wedding experience.

**Cons:**

- High price tag potentially makes it one of the more expensive destination wedding choices.
- The desert climate means extreme heat for much of the year, limiting outdoor activities to cooler months.

**Who It's For:**

- Couples seeking a glamorous and luxurious wedding experience in an urban setting. Ideal for those who want a modern wedding with the option to incorporate traditional Arabian elements and who appreciate the convenience and amenities of a cosmopolitan city.

## ❖ Maldives

**Pros:**

- It is synonymous with luxury and exclusivity, offering idyllic overwater venues that seem straight out of a dream.
- IPerfect for couples seeking privacy and romance.
- Offers unique opportunities for underwater wedding photos or ceremonies.

**Cons:**

- The exclusivity of the Maldives comes with a high cost, particularly for accommodations and dining.
- Its remote location can make travel logistics and planning more complex, and the reliance on imports can increase the overall cost of a wedding here.

**Who It's For:**

- Couples looking for an ultra-romantic, private island experience. The Maldives is ideal for those who envision a serene, beachfront ceremony with luxury at every turn, making it perfect for elopements or small, intimate gatherings.

## ❖ Napa Valley, California

**Pros:**
- Offers luxurious and intimate settings perfect for wine enthusiasts.
- The mild weather year-round is ideal for outdoor ceremonies.

**Cons:**
- Popular wedding destination, which can mean higher costs and the need to book well in advance.

**Who It's For:**
- Wine lovers and foodies who dream of a romantic wedding amidst rolling vineyards and exquisite culinary experiences.

## ❖ Aspen, Colorado

**Pros:**
- Ideal for winter weddings with a snowy backdrop, as well as beautiful summer mountain nuptials.
- Offers a range of outdoor activities for guests.

**Cons:**
- Can be expensive, particularly during peak ski season.
- Altitude may be a consideration for some guests.

**Who It's For:**

- Couples seeking a picturesque mountain setting, whether for a cozy winter wedding or a lush summer affair, and those who love outdoor adventures.

## ❖ Savannah, Georgia

**Pros:**

- The city's historic venues and moss-draped squares offer a picturesque and romantic setting.
- Relatively affordable compared to other destination wedding locales.

**Cons:**

- The hot and humid summer months can be uncomfortable for outdoor events.

**Who It's For:**

- Those enchanted by the allure of the Old South, seeking a wedding that combines historical elegance with the charm of a small city.

## ❖ Charleston, South Carolina

**Pros:**

- Offers a rich historical backdrop along with modern luxury.
- Known for its warm hospitality and charming venues.

**Cons:**

- Popular tourist and wedding destination, which can affect availability and prices.
- Summers can be hot and humid.

**Who It's For:**

- Couples drawn to the elegance and charm of the historic South, looking for a wedding that blends tradition with modern sophistication.

www.ingramcontent.com/pod-product-compliance
Lightning Source LLC
Chambersburg PA
CBHW060324050426
42449CB00011B/2637